The Poeming Pigeon
A Journal of Poetry & Prose

The Poeming Pigeon
A Literary Journal of Poetry

Volume 2, Issue 2
Poems about Music

A Publication of The Poetry Box®

©2016 The Poetry Box®
All rights reserved.
Each poem copyright reserved by individual authors.
Original Cover Illustration & Photographs by Robert R. Sanders.
Editing & Book Design by Shawn Aveningo Sanders.
Cover Design by Robert R. Sanders.
Printed in the United States of America.

No part of this book may be reproduced
in any matter whatsoever without written
permission from the author, except in the case
of brief quotations embodied in critical essays,
reviews and articles.

Library of Congress Control Number: 2016953116

ISBN-13: 978-0-9863304-6-9
ISBN-10: 09863304-6-9

Published by The Poetry Box®, 2016
Beaverton, Oregon
www.ThePoetryBox.com
530.409.0721

To music teachers worldwide
and those who work
to keep music in the schools —

this is our song for you!

Contents

Introduction	11
After the Big Bang ~*Michael T. Coolen*	15
Expansive Salvation ~*Scott Thomas Outlar*	16
Blessing X ~*Anne Whitehouse*	18
Street Music ~*Judith Skillman*	20
Blessed Wretch ~*Joanne Anglin*	21
Clangor of the Bell ~*Rosemary Douglas Lombard*	22
The soft edge of morning ~*Carolyn Martin*	23
Trio (3 Haiku) ~*Jack Maze*	24
Tree Top Tenor ~*Carolyn A. Dahl*	25
Große Fuge ~*Susan P. Blevins*	26
Bach's Coriolis ~*Claudia F. Savage*	28
A Familiar Song ~*Ada Jill Schneider*	30
Ashokan Farewell ~*Amy Miller*	31
On the Scent of a Tune ~*Diana Cole*	32
Song of the Katabatic Wind ~*Jennifer Fenn*	33
Clavicle Music ~*Judith Arcana*	34
Kithara's Lament ~*Suzanne DeWitt Hall*	35
Tuning the Piano ~*Wayne Lee*	36
Duet ~*Kate M. Wells*	37
A Neighbor's Music ~*Robert Coats*	38
Their Song ~*Marilyn Johnston*	39
Haydn at 4 A.M. ~*Alan Catlin*	40
Sestina on the Second Floor ~*Judith Barrington*	41
The Last Sonata, No. 32 in C Minor ~*Anne Harding Woodworth*	43
Luciano Pavarotti ~*Connie Post*	44
On Making Meatloaf while Maria Callas Sings *Care Nome* ~*Jane Miller*	46
Puccini, in Those Days ~*Gabrielle Brand*	47
First Songs ~*Deborah J. Meltvedt*	49
And Spit ~*Suzanne Bailie*	50

Summer's Siren Song ~Joan Leotta ... 51
My Son, Singing ~Linda Ferguson ... 52
Theory of Choir ~Annette L. Grunseth ... 53
The Day My High School Choir Director Dies ~Colette Tennant ... 55
For Joni ~Diane Elayne Dees ... 56
My Folk Song for You ~Tricia Knoll ... 57
Halftime at Woodstock ~Jennifer Hambrick ... 58
I Was a Teenage Disc Jockey ~Katy Brown ... 60
What We Thought We Heard ~Jan Haag ... 61
Prostrate ~Leah Mueller ... 62
Let it Be ~Connie Post ... 63
Abbey Road ~Nancy Haskett ... 65
B3 ... Boys, Band, Bus ~Sandra Hanks ... 67
Does She Ever Play Guitar? ~Eileen McGurn ... 68
He Breaks My Heart Like Loenard Cohen Did ~Karla Linn Merrifield ... 69
Wintry night, listening to Bolero ~Carol Taylor Was ... 70
The End Result of Rhythm and Blues ~Toni Partington ... 71
There Are More Verses to This Song ~Cynthia Linville ... 73
Empty Room Radio ~Julie Valin ... 74
Freebirds ~Todd Cirillo ... 75
This is What it Sounds Like ~A.J. Huffman ... 78
Forever 19 ~Shawn Aveningo ... 79
Nipples Up ~Sarah Key ... 80
Piazolla and Me ~Judith Kelly Quaempts ... 81
Dudamel at Disney Hall ~Peter Larsen ... 82
Falling in Love ~Jacqueline Jules ... 83
King of What? King of Who? ~Christopher Luna ... 84
Blues, 1961 ~Christopher Scribner ... 85
In Our Strange Home ~Julene Tripp Weaver ... 87
Little Boxes ~Lennart Lundh ... 90
Music isn't about standing still and playing it safe ~Bill Cushing ... 91
Betty Carter ~Akua Lezli Hope ... 94

Word Jazz ~Helen Kerner ... 95
Dispatches from the Microphone & Microphone Stand Perspective
~Janel Cloyd ... 97
Listening to *My Favorite Things* ~Orel Protopopescu ... 98
Moonwalker ~Mark Kerstetter ... 100
If Jimi Hadn't Died So Young ~Dan Raphael ... 101
Train Sounds ~David Belmont ... 103
Session Man ~Linda Goulden ... 104
Sax Axis ~Josh Gaines ... 105
Center, Fleeing ~Marj Hahne ... 107
On First Hearing the Voice of Joan Baez ~Peter D. Goodwin ... 108
Singing with Pete ~Jane Yolen ... 110
The Michigan Womyn's Music Festival ~Donna Barkman ... 111
Tracy Chapman ~David Jibson ... 112
Hit Song ~Jeffrey H. MacLachlan ... 113
At Marilyn's Backstreet Disco ~Shahé Mankerian ... 114
This Ain't No Disco ~Charles Rammelkamp ... 115
How to Write a Great Country Song ~Carolyn Martin ... 116
Karaoke Bar, Brooklyn ~Susana H. Case ... 117
La Música ~Lynn M. Knapp ... 118
The Singing Señoras of Guayabidos ~Bill Frayer ... 119
Cajun Bluegrass ~Brad G. Garber ... 120
Song from the Other Side ~Ellaraine Lockie ... 121
Father-Daughter Act ~Douglas Spangle ... 122
Music Heals ~Tiffany M. Burba ... 123
A Message in the Song ~Kathleen Corcoran ... 124
What But the Music ~Kenneth Salzmann ... 125
Acknowledgments ... 127
Contributors ... 129
Index of Poets (by last name) ... 141
About The Poetry Box® ... 145
Order Form ... 147

Introduction

> *Music is love in search of a word.*
> *~Sidney Lanier*
> *(American poet, musician)*

Poetry and music go together like peanut butter and jelly. But which came first? Some say music was born from poetry — an art form when performed aloud evolving into song. While some argue that poetry was born from music — the rhythmic movements providing basis for formal meter and rhyme. And like the proverbial egg and chicken, we can debate their origin or simply enjoy them both.

We begin our musically-inspired anthology exploring the origin of music through verse. Michael T. Coolen shares one theory in his poem, "After the Big Bang:"

> *the cosmic background radiation that was created*
> *resonates throughout the universe …*
> *… fifty-seven octaves below middle C*

while Scott Thomas Outlar takes a more spiritual approach to describing the origin of song in his poem, "Expansive Salvation:"

> *and the lyrics …*
> *found their way*
> *into the spirit of man*

My husband recently joined a band here in Portland. One day, his band mate Rich pronounced, "Music isn't created; it's a gift delivered from an unknown muse that can only be adapted, cultivated, shared and enjoyed." Regardless of your belief in Big Bang Theory or Creationism, one thing rings true — both music and poetry are a gift to us all.

Many of us have visceral connections to music — especially the music we listened to while coming of age. And while our musical tastes may differ greatly, there's a sort of universal magic that allows a song to trigger our most treasured memories. How many times have you found yourself driving down the road, radio blaring on your way to work or to pick the kids up from school, only to find yourself in another moment in time, catapulted by a song you remember from your youth? Suddenly you're slow-dancing in the gymnasium at a high school dance … or you're walking down the aisle … or you're looking up at your father while you dance on his toes. Music has the power to take you wherever you want to go (or go back to). Take for instance, "Bach's Coriolis," a formal poem by Claudia F. Savage:

> *The day's chaos moored into bass and treble, dark to light.*
> *I see his clouded face twenty-five years ago.*

Sometimes the memory is bittersweet. Reading through the piles of submissions, I was unexpectedly struck by a Susana H. Case's poem "Karaoke Bar, Brooklyn" and her reference to a song my grandma used to sing (slightly off-key) every time we rode in her car.

> *The mountain mama takes her turn*
> *on the stage, belts out*
> *Take me home, Country Roads*

Yes, singing along in the car — with or without the radio — is certainly a favorite pastime whether we're going on a family vacation or cruising with our friends. But how many times have you found yourself singing along to your favorite song only to later discover you've been singing the wrong lyrics all along? Check out the poem by Jan Haag titled, "What We Thought We Heard," and you'll chuckle at her misunderstood song lyrics:

> *On a dark desert highway, Cool Whip in my hair.*
> *Hold me closer, Tony Danza.*

Outside from the nostalgia aspect, music's importance to our social existence is paramount. After all, in 1977 when NASA created a time capsule to place aboard Voyager I — intended to communicate to extraterrestrials about human existence — they included musical selections ranging from Bach and Beethoven to Blind Willie Johnson and Chuck Berry. How ironic that Carl Sagan's suggestion for a Beatles' tune was omitted from the collection.

Music can be a double-edged sword having the power to divide us over our differences or unite us in a singular cause. On one hand it can lead us to war and even ignite a rage, as Alan Catlin's poem, "Haydn at 4 A.M." demonstrates:

> … Ah, the bombast and
> the pomp, that moved the men to unspeakable
> acts of unbearable cruelty …

On the other hand, it can direct us to work together in search of more peaceful solutions, as in the case of Peter Goodwin's poem, "On First Hearing the Voice of Joan Baez"

> *voices of passion*
> *voices of humor …*
> *voices that would create change*

By the time this book lands in the reader's hands, we will have reached the verdict in a monumental presidential election in the United States. Some will be happy with the outcome, and some will be disappointed. And after so many years of focusing on what divides us as a people, perhaps the best advice anyone could offer is found in our closing poem, "What But the Music" by Kenneth Salzmann:

> *What but the music might have bound us then?*
> *What but the music might bind us again?*

We hope you enjoy the poetic musical journey that lies on the pages that follow. May your soul be filled with music and your heart forever filled with song.

~ Shawn Aveningo Sanders
October, 2016

Michael T. Coolen

After the Big Bang

    instantly after the most recent Big Bang
    the universe we call ours inflated to a
    million
        million
            million
                million
                    million
                        times its initial size
    the number 1 with thirty zeroes after it

    in a fraction of a second the universe became
    an interconnected, continuous, homogenous entity where
    not a nova explodes
        not a black hole devours
            not a single electron moves
                not a pigeon falls from the sky
    but the universe knows this has happened

    the cosmic background radiation that was created
    resonates throughout the universe

    it is a D flat fifty-seven octaves below middle C
    it is the source of all music

Scott Thomas Outlar

Expansive Salvation

In the beginning ...

God's tongue
let loose
with the word Love,
and darkness
gave way to Light
as the radiant shine
of purified source
surged through the souls
of a thousand clay vessels,
breathing Life
into every lung
that longed to gasp
with an exclamation
of thankfulness.

Consciousness careened
through the infinite space
of an ethereal realm,
pulsing at every point
of a synchronized web
with notes
of harmonic vibration
as the song
of the spheres
burst with a bang
into an electric symphony
of static discharge,
and the lyrics
born from the stars
found their way

into the spirit of Man
as the perfect plan
reached a safe home
in which to rest.

Blessing X

I am keeping silent,
spending the summer day
in solitude in the country.
Listening to the birds call,
I recognize only a few.
How have I lived so long
without learning to name them?

I touch a porch column
and am caught in a spider's web.
Last night, in the porch light,
I watched one casting
such a vivid shadow
against the house I thought
I was seeing double.
I couldn't spot the web at night,
but I watched the dance that made it,
the spider flinging itself across space,
catching itself on a thread,
spinning out more,
its forelegs knitting rapidly
as it braced itself for the next leap.

At the top point of the barn roof,
the wasps have built a nest.
I watch them fly in and out.

   * *

I am thinking of Eleanor
who lived here twenty-eight years,
first with Mark, then without him.
When she was alive,

piano music issued from this house
for several hours every day,
louder in summer
when the windows were flung open,
but also in winter,
muffled by panes of glass,
sinking soft as lamplight
on the snow.

A house with music is a blessing.
For Eleanor, cursed by deafness,
music came to live inside her.
Through a great effort of will,
she listened with her fingers.
How she did it I do not know,
but I watched her succeed
at the end of her long, blessed life.
Her love of the art
and the instrument,
the pleasure she took
in its difficulty and mastery
kept her at it day after day.
She surrounded herself
with images of angels.
Her abiding wish
was to instruct by delight.

Judith Skillman

Street Music

At five o'clock the fishmen take back their ice.

One by one
      the long tables empty,
           cleared of dried flowers,
                vegetables,
and hashish pipes shaped like the starship enterprise.

The harp played by a blind woman who stared into the sun,
      her eyes changing like water.

JoAnn Anglin

Blessed Wretch

It's not my church anymore, but old motions come
back to me and I catch on to the ones they've changed.
I take my father to Saturday evening mass. Whatever

the music, the gruff voice is strong, sounds sweet to me.
Once, we never sang *Amazing Grace*, but the Catholics
adopted it and he knows it by heart, by soul. I think

he carries grace in his marrow, but I know he's been
tempted and I recall the period of trouble between
him and my mom, their ten years of wounded sorrow,

unhealed betrayal. He kneels creakily in the pews, can
no longer take up the collection – unsteady legs. He was
known for the firmness of his word; to many, his goodness

shone and he was relied on. Now he sometimes gets
lost, cannot find his way home, feels unsafe. He counts
his sins worse than others do and in his time of fewer

days, he hopes for even more grace to appear. No longer
a shield to me; it's what I've become to him. But tonight he
sings full of faith, of being found, of overflowing grace.

Rosemary Douglas Lombard

Clangor of the Bell

> *Hark how the bells, sweet silver bells,*
> *All seem to say, throw cares away.*
> *Ding dong, ding dong.*
> *~ Peter Wilhousky*

Harkened to the bedlam of yet another day
by the belligerent clanking of that damn bell,
I say, awakened by the bell not so sweet,
can't they leave a poor beldam's ears in peace?

You say a bell is a bell is a bell? Oh, no.
Bells can tinkle, ding, resound, or dong,
their sonorities smooth and rich as fine chocolate.

But this one? its sound too strident, cacophonous,
its metal to metal grating my ears, like
a two-year-old banging and clanging the pots —
I cannot bear another day of discordant alarms.

I must plan. The door to the abbey is left unlocked.
I'll rise after matins and vest in black.
What are the odds of my failing?

The belfry is high and I am old, but I am strong
as well and bold enough. No harms
will be done when I capture that clapper,
let it down at the end of the bell rope, and throw cares away!

At daybreak this beldam will watch the bell swing
as the bellman again pulls the end of the rope —
my only hope: that I'll not swing in hell for my content,

for the clangorous bell, come the dawn, will be silent;
and only I, save God, will know where its clapper has gone.

Carolyn Martin

The soft edge of morning

and "On Eagles Wings" glides
up the stairs. Feathering
piano keys, you soprano
verses and refrains.
And I will bear you up ... you sing.

Music becomes you, my dear,
and ... *makes you ... shine like the sun ...*
warming squirrels and jays
playing in our Douglas firs.
Even feral cats pause on the patio
and the neighbor's dog stops his yap.
They recognize the words.

I translate this space
into scribbled lines:
*When the wind's too weak
to raise our sails,
we'll guide each other home.*

Between notes and words,
quibbles and making up,
we abide – solid/subtle/bold.
... *and I will hold you,* you sing.

"Beautiful," I whisper to myself
and mouth the final words —
knowing them as well as you —
... *in the palm of My hand.*

Trio

wind through the trees
leaves a song sung by dead wood —
last year's fire

***

your gentle voice
the music that makes it all
worthwhile

***

musical notes
freed from a score, now in flight —
birds leaving their roost

Carolyn Dahl

Tree Top Tenor

Singing his arias from the top
of a red bud tree like a tenor
hoping to shatter glass, I unplug
my earphones and listen to his
mockingbird riff of blue jay,
cardinal, woodpecker stutter.
The way he struts his songs,
though hawks circle nearby,
makes me wonder: when
did I lose the courage to sing?

I remember warbling in front
of an old piano, plinking the ivories,
pumping my lungs to *Natural Woman*,
delirious with notes and reasons to sing.
When did I grow silent, believe music
no longer requires a throat?
The gray bird doesn't peck an app,
nor download the Top Ten Avian Tunes,
though he is a Napster of birds' songs.

When he rewinds his song book
memory and without changing
feathers, trills an oriole, I shape
my soft lips to the point of a beak,
find my voice behind my teeth,
and scat-sing with the bird.
My husband rushes from
the house, binoculars dangling
from his neck, and searches
the tree for a strange, new bird
he has never heard.

Susan P. Blevins

Große Fuge

Here I am, sixty-eight and
I just had a musical first

Last night a revelation of
music made visible

Quartet on fire
They the alchemists that
transformed sound into music
and music into visible art

Hovering sheets and waves of color
moved and shifted with the notes

Northern Lights of harmonies
swayed before my eyes
Hanging curtains of visible sound

Finally I have seen the
music of the spheres

Transfixed I watched the swathe of
rich eggplant purple painted before my eyes
with powerful Van Gogh strokes —
Beethoven's color

Impertinent rhythm of the
gigue coquetted its way
across the page and
across my auditory landscape

Shards of blinding silver
notes climbing ever higher

Splash of red, dark green
daubs of gold and ochre

Geometry of black lines designed the
architecture of this amazing fugue

My eyes and ears merged to listen and see
this prophetic work unfold
My soul united with the mystery unlocked
all around me

I am at one with Beethoven
at one with his ecstasy of exaltation

Atonement

Claudia F. Savage

Bach's Coriolis*
~ after Linda Pastan

My father wanted to be music.
Tonight, I play the *Goldberg Variations* after dinner.
The day's chaos moored into bass and treble, dark to light.
I see his clouded face twenty-five years ago.

I play the *Goldberg Variations* after dinner.
Fingers desperate to weave what my voice cannot.
I see his clouded face twenty-five years ago.
Closed eyes, head swaying with the crescendo's wind.

Desperate to weave what my voice cannot
I heave everything toward beauty.
Closed eyes, head swaying with the crescendo's wind.
My ribs turn canyons.

Everything toward beauty.
History be damned. I weave peace with my fingers.
My ribs turn canyons.
My heart pneumatic with arpeggio.

It was always after dinner, my fingers desperate
To keep up with Glenn Gould.
Till my veins possessed the hum of fugue.
Till the record needle stalled, beaten.

Keeping up with Glenn Gould,
Twenty-five years ago, I closed my eyes.
After dinner, at the piano, in striped pajamas.
To make his face still, his hands listening.

My ribs turned canyons.
The day's chaos moored into bass and treble, dark to light.
My heart pneumatic with arpeggio.
My father, desperate to be music.

* The reeling gyroscopic effect of the earth's spin that creates wind and flow of weather.

A Familiar Song

Swaying in slow motion or rewinding
the old words in your mind? Which
comes first when you hear a familiar song?

Maybe the one you remember
hearing over the radio in 1943
when air-raid sirens screamed *black-out night*
and Mama pulled every window shade
tight-to-the-sill and shut off every light.

There'll be bluebirds over
the white cliffs of Dover.
Tomorrow, just you wait and see.

Did you listen for Messerschmitts to fly over
as you hid under your chenille bedcover?
Did you pray for the war to be over?
When Mama turned the lights back on,
was the war over?

Amy Miller

Ashokan Farewell

By the third note,
it's a whine — the slide
up to D like the creak
of the old front door or the oven
I opened with a dishcloth, slow.
All the openings: the back yard
onto the creek, a song
trying to match the wind, hilltops
speaking no human name,
the shed up the rise with birch
piled under the eaves, black scent
of motor oil. Winter
beat us senseless, pushed us
into a warm corner of the bed,
bow and fingers dragged with mute
and slur, then sometimes bright —
yes, that's right, there are other
ways to remember this:
Yes, some mornings sang
like coffee poured in hungry cups.

Diana Cole

On the Scent of a Tune

Can you name it ... that scent
rising up from the piano?
If I put my nose into it
it doesn't knock me out like Tchaikovsky
with his rose parade, or pepper
my sinuses like a Bach toccata.

I first noticed the scent of music,
a Puccini opera to be exact,
at the outdoor stadium in Verona —
hand-held candles burning down
to the down beat, a darkening sky,
a whiff, then bar after bar of milk chocolate.

I couldn't stop, not even in church
when Poulenc let out a thunderous fart,
his fine art of colliding harmonies.
Street corners reeked of electrical fire —
Juan Atkins, Cybotron and Wire
burning up the beat.

To this day I can't smell incense
without a Gregorian chant
widening my nostrils.
And licorice, I hate it.
It hangs all over the Muzak
secreting from every store.

But this riff is elusive,
a jig that stirs up Jambalaya
a sprig pressed, packed away
but aired out tonight.
Cloud after cloud like
(sneeze) ... ragtime!

Jennifer Fenn

Song of the Katabatic Wind
A haibun

We step onto the top layer of ancient ice, our footprints becoming the latest notes to the song of the katabatic wind.

    The first notes sounded
    eons past with snow falling,
    pianissimo.

We hear the wind blow across the blue and white vastness, crystals still glistening despite years of footsteps.

    Like faraway drums,
    the First Nations' sturdy feet
    crossed over this ice.

The wind whistles in whispery echoes through the misty white veil surrounding the snow-frosted Rocky Mountains. It calls us to stand still and listen closely.

    Blowing all alone,
    poetic melancholy
    resounds through the ages.

Back on our snowmobile, we crane our necks for one last farewell look at the far-reaching field of ice, leaving the wind to sing its eternal song.

    Alone on the ice,
    with only mountains to hear,
    glacial winds sing on.

Judith Arcana

Clavicle Music

Between wings of bone
the throat's heart opens
to blue-beating pulse —
composing in small chambers
blood songs for ancient instruments.

 Suzanne DeWitt Hall

Kithara's Lament

I wait with my sister
my twin
for him to come.

He walks through the door
and moves toward us.

I wonder;
will it be me?

He picks her up
pulls her into his lap
caressing her curves
cradling her neck
and begins to play.

His hands move across her strings
pressing, plucking, strumming
as music fills the air.

My strings respond to each chord
vibrating, resonating,
humming subtly
hollowness yearning to be filled
to be played
to sing along
to feel the wonder of the music-maker's touch.

I hum
and wait in hope
for the someday that will come
when he who plays
will fill me with song.

And I will sing.

Wayne Lee

Tuning the Piano

It's an old-fashioned craft
striking again and again
the 88 keys
up and back
endless chords and scales
octaves and arpeggios
hitting a hammer
turning a peg
then plunking once again
the ebony or ivory

and listening
always listening
trusting what is true.

It's a disappearing art
this belief in the ear
this faith
that your instrument
is perfectly pitched
for the world.

Kate M. Wells

Duet

After a year of Twinkle Little Star,
she graduated to minuets, gavottes, bourrées.
Recitals at the church, floor length gowns.
Her hair, inexpertly French-braided by her mother.

When she learned her first Beethoven
the family went to Luby's Cafeteria.
Beethoven to Vivaldi,
Dvorak to Tchaikovsky.
Her parents saved a year
and for graduation — an $800 violin,
new case, old bow, extra strings
and fancy rosin in the flannel cloth.

Chin to shoulder,
she played through training
for her Western Union job, three children,
community orchestra.

Pensions, prescriptions and far away
children calling on the holidays.
Rehearsals every Wednesday night
in the high school gym.

Tonight, she curls around her violin,
chin to shoulder, and plays.
Fingers hammer against string,
and the creases stay in her skin.

Robert Coats

A Neighbor's Music

Walking the dog late
on a damp winter night
I hear music, follow it to the house
of Mrs. Wimmer. German *lieder*,
on a scratchy 78:
"... *mein liebe Schatz ... ein Vogelsang ...*"

What memories might such a song evoke
in a woman of 95?
Of a time before jackboots,
before the Western Front.
Perhaps of a park in Vienna,
children in sailor suits,
men fishing on a riverbank ....

For a moment I want to knock on her door,
to hear her stories of love, loss,
and struggle in a new country.
But of course I don't. The dog
gives her collar a toss.
We continue up the sidewalk,
"*ein Vogelsang*" with piano
fading behind us into the still air.

Marilyn Johnston

Their Song

My husband told me about a guy in his unit
named Eddie, a mechanic from East Tennessee.
He said he had gotten married the day before
shipping out for Vietnam. Eddie carried around
"You've Lost that Lovin' Feelin'" on a cassette tape,
said it was their favorite song, and he played
it over and over in the six-man tent —
all the newly-arrived grunts housed
in their temporary camp south of Duc Pho.

Somehow not one of them ever screamed
at Eddie to shut the damn thing off or threatened
to take the tape and bash it to smithereens.

After their platoon's search and destroy missions,
Eddie would return and wait for mail call,
for the letters that never came.
Still, day after day, he played the same song —
Bill Medley and Bobby Hatfield's deep,
melodic voices spilling out through the tent
while the others lay back on their cots,
breathing to the beat of their own fears,
feeling the weight of each other's losses.

Haydn at 4 A.M.

Windblown snow and ice against
the cracked third floor window.
Classical music on the radio; grace
and static fighting the white noise
inside for supremacy. Haydn and
Mozart, almost Germans, the Nazis
hated, because they lacked the kind
of drama that would send impressionable
young men to war to die for a morally
bankrupt cause. Ah, the bombast and
the pomp, that moved the men to unspeakable
acts of unbearable cruelty. Wagner, Orff,
Schreker, conducted by von Karajan and
Klemperer, father of Werner, Colonel
Klink the ludicrous Kommandant of
Hogan's Heroes; nothing funny about
a stalag in real life. No one ever
associated blood libel or lust with
Eine Kleine Nachtmusik. No one
felt Bach's *Devil's Chord* the way
they felt the *Ride of the Valkyrie's*.
In *Apocalypse Now* Robert Duvall
as Lieutenant Colonel Kilgore said
"The men love it." as he launched
a gunship raid on an unsuspecting
Vietnamese village. Kilgore was
not exactly a Nazi but he had a weird aura
that made him almost as crazy as one.
Think of all the dead people they would
leave behind, and the music they would
no longer hear.

Judith Barrington

Sestina On The Second Floor

She tied herself tight with a washing line
at shoulders and hips to a dining chair's straight back.
Eight hours, sometimes nine, she practiced
scales, arpeggios, notes to strengthen her fingers,
sometimes a phrase by Bach over and over
till everyone else in the house wanted to scream.

I can't understand why she, too, didn't scream
but seemed content to work for hours on that line,
trying to find the grace as her fingers ran over
the yellowing keys of the baby grand. Her back
held straight by rope, her mind in her fingers,
up on the second floor, my sister practiced —

and I, in the garden listened while I practiced
climbing the crab apple tree. Mother would scream
so I'd slither down, bark burning my fingers,
or save myself by grabbing the knotty clothesline.
Preludes and fugues, etudes, still carry me back
when I set them to play at random over and over.

My sister left and I was supposed to take over
the ebony piano stool but I rarely practiced
playing only on Sundays when she came back:
thumping duets, spooning chocolate ice cream,
we'd argue about the rhythm of a tricky line
but truthfully I couldn't keep up with her fingers.

Now, years later, she pulls out a score and fingers
dog-eared pages. Reading the stave, she goes over
the piano part, each note familiar, each line
clear in her mind. Her chamber group has practiced
enough, though the cellist makes her want to scream
when he comes in late and they all must go back

to the top of the page and do it over again. In the back
of her mind does she wonder how long her fingers —
the joints swollen and red — will bend? Does the scream
inside her almost erupt till she flips it over
like the page with its corner creased up? She's practiced
keeping her fears at bay, the musical line

always in front, the line of her life pushed back.
Long ago she practiced over and over,
her fingers joyful. Now each note hides a scream.

Anne Harding Woodworth

The Last Sonata, No. 32 in C Minor
~ for Nina, who is losing her hearing

Eventually Beethoven didn't hear
his own music, and likewise your ears
are cheating you, though you hear well enough

to smile. You hear well enough to know
the melodies. You hear well enough
to take something from this concert hall.

Once, you sat in a tiny rocker, while
she played this very sonata. You absorbed
the sounds then in the way only a child listens.

Tomorrow you will hum a few cadences
into the phone — a real hum with the muscles
of your tongue, throat, and neck — to tell her

where you've been. She will not disappoint you.
Like any mother, she will identify the sounds
that entered into you tonight.

She cannot play them anymore,
but some sounds never fade, even when
they barely reach the inner ear.

Connie Post

Luciano Pavarotti
(1935–2007 ~ San Francisco Chronicle)

In the last moments —
did all the crumbs of lost notes
fall beneath the table

Did every aria run through his veins
until his breath was like
an ovation
extended, longed for

When his eyes were closed
did his music flow like
cream on the underside
of his marrow

Did he stand in front of thousands
again
holding his hands high
the applause flowering
at his feet

or, as the lights faded
like an old lantern
did he remember
that he was the son of a baker
go back to the days
when they sang together
in a modest church

Did he remember
as he departed
that bread was rising
and falling

being broken and
and passed

countless loaves
leavening
steam
all over the windows

Jane Miller

On Making Meatloaf while Maria Callas Sings
Care Nome

The trees on the rug perk
their flowered ears, the graceful plant
by the lamp leans in, my children
still children in pictures watch me, bowl in lap.
My hand dutifully mixing
stills and all her hopeful notes
rise into air and then fall, hesitant
then more sure, note
chasing note, the orchestra,
an anxious suitor, stumbling after.
Birds from watercolor landscapes burst
winter trees and barn loft
to join her love as it trills and rests, its descant
indenting sofa cushions. As men chorus
offstage, the globe by the desk inclines
its world-weariness. She does not hear
their warning or see the dog's fluffy dragon toy
slain at my feet. Crying, I stir the raw meat
into its binder of egg and bread crumbs.

Gabriella Brand

Puccini, in Those Days

Even when I was a toddler, I loved my Puccini.
Pooo chee nee. Pooo chee nee.

"She wants to come for a listen" Grandfather would say,
yielding to my outstretched hands.

While the rest of the family sat around the dinner table,
everyone nursing the strong LaVazza, the women (in those days)
refilling the cups,
I'd be carried out to the living room, to the velvet sofa, to the rows of
records lining the walls.

"What's that? "Grandpa would ask, pointing to his ancient Victrola,
its bulbous cornucopia, the little dog logo.

Pooo chee nee. Pooo chee nee.

Grandpa would put a record on, newly vinyl (in those days) and we'd
settle in. He'd put one arm around me like a shawl, the thin smoke
of his Camel cigarette curling through my hair, the smell of tobacco
mingling with baby powder. I'd stick my thumb in my mouth and fall
asleep.

Later, at eight or nine, I looked forward to the same ritual, Grandpa and
I on the sofa, Puccini between us like an old friend.

By then, I knew every scratch, every hesitation,
the crescendo of poor Butterfly left waiting,
the minor key of Mimi coughing in the night,
the arpeggios of longing and loss.

Sometimes the old man would close his eyes and doze,
not even awakening when the record needle began to wander towards

the paper label.
Tosca's last leaping cry just a whisper in his mind.
By then, I'd learned to gingerly take Puccini off the spindle by myself,
and place him back in his cardboard sleeve, like tucking in a child
for the night.

I'd tiptoe out of the room, my heart a little wider,
the world a little softer.
(In those days)

Deborah J. Meltvedt

First songs

The first songs you won't remember.
They were sung before
your lungs hit air and vocal cords woke up.
Through underwater cord
you sucked chords —
as vital as iron
as needed as oxygen,
the whispered lilt of lullaby
a big brother's drum screams,
chop sticks in between piano lessons,
your mother's voice sewing your bones.

Suzanne Bailie

And Spit

Chu ga Chu ga Chu ga Chu ga

Again!

How do we ask?

Please. Again!

Back button on the CD player, press.

The stirring Rafi song promoting

nightly brushing to be more than a

quick lick of the toothpaste tube is now,

a Top 10, toddler mesmerizer,

afternoon listening, mandatory finger motion,

driving home from daycare music

favorite.

The verse begins ...

When you get up in the morning and it's

Quarter to one and you want to have a little fun

You brush your teeth

Chu ga Chu ga Chu ga Chu ga

You brush your teeth

Chu ga Chu ga Chu ga Chu ga

Joan Leotta

Summer's Siren Song

My cousins and I commanded
Grandma's porch
on summer evenings where
we played and waited for cool
breezes to push away
the heat of day.
My older cousin Jamie
sometimes practiced fiddle.
When he left the fiddle home
we contented ourselves with
cricket serenades as background
for our reading, talking
and epic Monopoly tournaments.
On the other side of the porch
grownups played cards,
talked, and listened to the radio.
Patiently we all awaited
night's star performance.
It came from the street —
a siren song, that
emptied porches all around.
Grown-ups and children alike,
we poured down driveways
and leapt through lawns
as soon as we heard its enticing tune —
the song of the ice cream truck.

Linda Ferguson

My Son, Singing

You take your place
in the college choir
beneath the dome
of a sky-blue ceiling —
you, blending your baritone
with the gleaming layers
of soprano, tenor and bass,
all combining to make a sound so rich
I can imagine Mozart himself,
robed in silk and spinning genius,
offering this concert
to the gods and goddesses.
In such a sea of resplendence,
your copper hair is sunlight
shining through stained glass,
and my love for you has become
a gleaming cathedral
where your voice
(through all of time,
a music made by you
alone) reverberates
in my bones.

Annette L. Grunseth

Theory of Choir
(Why Choir is Essential)

It's the breathing,
we go deep
to push notes upward.
The diaphragm
does its proper job,
restoring balance after we
limp in for rehearsal
beaten down by
the shallow breathing of rushing
from one thing to the next.
We focus on music, this night,
the ebb and flow of dynamics, text,
breathing, and more breathing,
where nothing else could possibly
clutter our heads except
the lissom line of black notes
running up and down the page,
and words catching us off our guard
as we press the two together
turning both into music.
Singing transposes us from
demanding bosses,
final exams,
ridiculous deadlines,
that nagging pain in the small curve of the back.
We are made whole again in music.
We seek the rhythm of our hearts,
find harmony in the sum of our parts.
We chant our stories
one note, upon another and another,
we blend as one, a collective "everyone"
sitting side by side, row upon row.

Like bricks on a path,
carefully laid down
one next to the other,
one journey of sound
one interlocking message,
as we crescendo upward,
assembled at the seam of Here
and the Hereafter,
our scores held firmly to our chests.

Colette Tennant

The Day My High School Choir Director Dies

I'll remember his crescendos —
what one metal music stand
could become in his hands —
a high hat cymbal, castanets,
a crude spear thrown
mostly toward the baritones.

I'll remember singing
The water is wide,
I cannot get o'er,
and neither have I
wings to fly.

By then, he'll know all about them —
the wide water, the crossing,
the wings.

Diane Elayne Dees

For Joni

The canyons echo the coyote's mournful cry
of loneliness, for which there are no words,
yet suddenly, like graceful home-bound birds,
the words appear as written on the sky.
The painted ponies dip, then leap so high,
they startle us. In silver-bridled herds,
they bear us through the grand and the absurd;
at journey's end, we still do not know why.
And yet the music calls us to go on,
amid an often misty atmosphere
that tends to blur the darkness and the light.
The melodies remain after we've gone,
as glorious reminders we were here,
though we are stardust scattered in the night.

Tricia Knoll

My Folk Song for You

If I had a microphone, a voice fit for singing,
or an acoustic guitar, I'd sing my folk song
about you. How I saw you last week sitting
on cardboard by the Nike store on the bus mall.
Gray hair. Gray beard. Your face
a tinge of green, lips thin like envelopes.

Fingerless gloves and a watch cap.
Were you shivering? It was damp enough
that your cardboard sign bowed.
Your blue eyes met mine. I knew you.

I never saw your name
in reunion planning emails.
I hadn't thought of you
for fifty years
until that rainy Saturday.
The last time I saw you
was on the bleachers
at our high school field

for end-of-season baseball.
Not a championship game
Warriors would win. Not that year
or for many years to come.

How you and I stood,
and sang
the national anthem
side by side.

Jennifer Hambrick

Halftime at Woodstock

    band geek trotting deep field
    teachers in bleachers
    crunching popcorn
    cheering attaboys
    thick-rimmed glasses
    cool kids cutting classes
    and your clarinet marches
    to a different beat
    knees-up double time
    outta line cris-cross
    trumpets trombones xylophones
    cut loose on *Purple Haze*
    daze the crowd
    with groovy howls
    animal growls
    psychedelic trills
    football grill turns
    Yasgur's farm
    uniform goes funky fringe
    Q-Tip hat wraps flat
    around your head
    marching band Jimi
    smack that clarinet
    behind your back
    your Black Beauty
    now a star singing
    moaning groaning
    over pompom frenzy
    buzzing above
    quarterback smack
    shaking quaking
    its dream song

with the coolest
badest-ass Aquarian cats
around.

Katy Brown

I Was a Teenage Disc Jockey

Can you call it an audition, if
you don't want the job?
I was wrong in every way. But,
somebody needed to start the try-outs
and I was tricked into the reading.

A nerdy geek, the darkroom and camera
were my tools. Broadway cast recordings
played on my home phonograph.
While others twisted at the sock-hops,
I dodged and cropped black&white pix.
Not my gig: the world of pop.

Or, so I thought.
A disembodied voice gives little away
as to the life-details of a radio jockey.
The listener can't see *Hello, Dolly!*
and *Funny Girl* on your home turntable;
can't smell darkroom fixer on your fingers.

Apparently, I sounded like a tall, thin cheerleader
— if you've never seen me.
I listened to every pop song that summer:
both the hit-side and the obscure B-side.
And for 9 months, I knew the words
to every song on the radio.

Before that reluctant audition,
if you'd asked me about the British Invasion,
I'd have said it was in 1776 in New York.
My senior year marked me forever, musically.
To this day, I can sing-along every word
with the oldies (from 1964-65).

Jan Haag

What We Thought We Heard
(misunderstood song lyrics)

On a dark desert highway, Cool Whip in my hair.
Hold me closer, Tony Danza.
Count the head lice on the highway.
You might as well face it, you're a dick with a glove.
Because sweet dreams are made of cheese.
Donuts make my brown eyes blue.
I've got two chickens to paralyze.
It's the age of asparagus.
The ants are my friends, they're blowin' in the wind.
Do you like bean enchiladas?
I like big butts and a can of limes.
Like a virgin, touched for the thirty-first time.
The sheep don't like it — rock the catbox, rock the catbox.
You walked into the potty like you were walking onto a yacht.
Theeeeeere's a bathroom on the right.
Joy to the visions that the people see.
Goodbye, aubergine.
I'll never leave your pizza burnin'.

Prostrate

    Lying on the floor
        between the stereo speakers
   wormhole notes
      fill my head, sink in
   clumsy waves to bone.
The music carries my ears
      skyward, and the rest of
   me sprawls immobile on the floor,
       arms spread wide in surrender.
One car passes
      in the street below, backfires
slightly as it coughs for gas
        and I almost don't notice,
as I drown in the warm chocolate
        intervals of silence,
   the sticky pauses
     that lead effortlessly
            to sound.

Connie Post

Let it Be

When I was nine
Paul McCartney's voice
seeped through the bottom cracks
of all the doors in the house

"When I find myself in times of trouble"
how a young girl plays
the same music in her room
as if the singer knows
her name
her crumpled, simple thoughts

"Mother Mary comes to me"
how a young girl
believes the man inside
the record player knows
when she is taking off her dress

"Whisper words of Wisdom"
how a man's voice can understand
there is no mother
no words
no rosary bead
sturdy enough for this heavy a prayer

"Let it Be, Let it Be"
and she does
Let it be, only to let it fall
as she swallows the rosary
the beads, the cross
the song

and it crumbles
like the lyrics
that broke in her hand
upon learning
how to leave a room

Nancy Haskett

Abbey Road

I.
My granddaughters think it's some kind of magic,
how I know which song comes next —
that *Something* follows *Come Together,*
how *Golden Slumbers* morphs right into *Carry that Weight* —
the way I can sing the upcoming notes before they are played,
how I know almost every word from every track by heart;
maybe someday they'll play one of their CDs over and over,
one hundred times, two hundred times,
like we played that record in the fall of '69,
the early months of '70,
down in the church basement,
the one we converted into a "coffee house" called the Free Spirit,
spent hours playing pool with that album on the phonograph,
finished Side One *I Want You,*
flipped it over *Here Comes the Sun,* again and again
so that now, in my car over forty-five years later,
when the songs play I hear the echoes of billiard balls
click and knock together —
the background accompaniment
of percussive apparitions

II.
The studio and crosswalk are still here,
but the painted lines are different now,
and it's a busy street;
everyone waits until it's clear in both directions,
steps out and walks to the opposite corner,
tries to picture the album cover —
first John in white suit and tennis shoes,
Ringo in black with boots,
Paul barefoot, cigarette in his right hand,
George last in denim blue.

We cross the street today
and despite all the years and changes,
there is a connection,
a contentment

knowing we are here
where they were

B3 ... Boys, Band, Bus

Oh! That time
I went to dance
and the band played *More*
because life is long
at sixteen and seventeen
at sixes and sevens

Oh! That time
we were dead certain
Love Is a Beautiful Thing
so fell in head first
like the water was warm
and we were buoyant

Oh! That time
when backs were strong
a B3 was a feather
music went on forever
dancing all night long
a lifetime guarantee

Oh! That time
a VeeDub was a bus
sharing space with a snare
heaving hormones on the hoof
the horse agrees
we carry on

Oh! That time
so distant / near
half a century spins out
shreds of threads
woven tightly through fabric
just slightly richer

Does She Ever Play Guitar?

Every rocker, every rapper, every punk
Has a big-eyed, long-limbed girl.
She dresses in black
And her innocence surrounds her
Like perfume.
When he plays
She sits alone at the table
Delicately folding and refolding a napkin.
Her eyes reach for him
As though he is a life raft
And she is slipping under
Rough water.

Karla Linn Merrifield

He Breaks My Heart Like Leonard Cohen Did

What is it with music men?
Their secret language of genius.
Their enchanting fractional rune-notes gathered
in compositions as if by gifted shamans — I listen
to their galaxy's stars scatter from each one's staff
among eighth, quarter, half, and whole moons.
On guitar, on piano, they perform the alchemy
of Erato's intensity stirred with Euterpe's dense desire.
A single chord from their fingers is a nebula.
They touch my ears with novae.

Carol Taylor Was

Wintry night, listening to Bolero

    the slow voice of flute
               is a ruffle of blue silk
      and your lover whispers
in your ear   down your neck
             along the shoulder
    woodwinds are the sigh   of feathers
  awakening your spine
       as the movement unwinds
   from an unhurried spool
of sound
        barely audible
           it's a hidden stream trickling
   where soft wings flutter
      repeat
score upon score   then quivering chords
    build in high-pitched notes
  of clarinet   piccolo
      the echo
connects *dolce*   with desire   bodies
  thirsty as tongues
      humming   on slippery skin
        plum ripe
tempo climbs   voice over voice
  oboe and bass clarinet   deliberate
     piercing pitch
the crescendo ignites   pulse pounding
    snare drums   on and on
  the rhythm   and volume louder
     louder   kettle drums strike
  drenched
        in the flourish

Toni Partington

The End Result of Rhythm and Blues

Marvin Gaye pleads *Sexual Healing*
for thousands of broken hearts
>*Baby I'm hot just like an oven*
>*I need some lovin'*

Then, spoken deep, sultry
>*Isn't that nice?*
>*I mean really, when you really sit and think about it*
>*isn't it really, really nice?*

thousands of babies conceived by
the end of Barry White's song

Rhythm and Blues is just the medicine
>when passion flees the bedroom
>when appetites are curbed by church hymns
>when the preacher raises his voice; demands
>that you banish those lurid thoughts

That's not the gospel of Reverend Al, no
>*Just you take your time, no hurry baby*
>*Sing low and take it slow*
>*Then, Lay it down, let it go, fall in love*

R&B explodes when James Brown
>calls for Hot Pants
>and grown men
>want grown women
>inside the pleasure dome
>some delicious funk-a-delic dessert

>when Joni says, *sex kills*
>I say, sex thrills – makes
>a harlot with no shame

for biological imperatives

all lit up by Motown Fuel
until fire under a skin dance
waits for sweet sweat
to cool it down

Cynthia Linville

There Are More Verses to This Song

Adagio
This curve
Your tongue on my cheek
Accelerando
This hand
Your fingers in my mouth
Allegro
This skin
Your heart pounding against my thigh
Da Capo
Touch
Take
Give me
Please
Espressivo
Now —
Your mouth opens
Your eyes glaze
Your breath moistens
Fermata . . .
The needle is stuck in the final groove:
you you you you you

Julie Valin

Empty Room Radio

You are my favorite song
that hasn't come on in years,
the one I'd dance in the car to,
or play while chopping onions
with the steady beat
and a wild trumpet solo.

I am Nina Simone, enticing:
Do I move you,
are you willin?
Do I groove you, is it thrillin'?

I am BB's Lucille,
my soul strummed and bent,
ringing out, filling every corner
of the space you stand in,
long after
I've walked away.

I am 3AM blues,
Koko Taylor's Voodoo Woman,
I can look through water, and see dry land.
I'm looking through water now, and
can still make out your face.
I swear,
you're smiling.

I am the radio left on
in an empty room,
my hopeful notes
plucking the curtains
with the kiss of a harmonica,
a chorus of pleas.

Todd Cirillo

Freebirds
~ *a mix-tape*

It begins with a Bukowski fall,
hard on the high hopes
and plenty of human heartache
with Bob Seger nights
that move to the sound
of all the leaves turning brown
which make us wish we were
in California
riding that Coltrane Blue Train
up and down the coast
through fog and
pleasant valley Sunday's

moving into a Miles Davis winter,
cold but clean
spending long Jimi Hendrix evenings
with me standing next to
your fire
singing Aretha's soul serenade
until we wake up
to Neil Young singing,
"be on my side
and I'll be on your side."
and then —
here comes the sun
in springtime
full of Booker T Bar-B-Ques
with Jefferson Airplane
blossoming in the backyard
and Sly just keeps taking us higher
into Allman Brother dreams
of twisted weekends

in New Orleans
hanging with you and the Meters
while Professor Longhair
cooks out back
dancing a Sinatra slow dance
up the Mississippi
under Elvis' blue moon of Kentucky.
Into a Tom Waits summertime
livin easy with Janis & the Isley Brothers
packing all our hopes and Bobby McGee dreams
into a straight no chaser road trip
with Thelonius Monk
stopping only at the greasiest truck stops
of chicken fried steak
with a side order of strange fruit
served by Billie Holiday.

We can spend the night
chasing the devil
with Jerry Lee Lewis'
great balls of fire
while drinking Tennessee whiskey
with Waylon Jennings
and meeting the Doors at the end
like Robin Trower,
too rolling stoned
to make it home.
Beginning the next day
in Willie's Bloody Mary morning
singing road songs,
you driving my truck
like Johnny Cash on a bender
giving me that sweet emotion of Aerosmith
under the sign reading Highway 61

and when the last dance
has been saved for us

I will give you my heart
while Grand Funk Railroad
takes us closer to home
that higher ground Stevie Wonder talks about
and we fall into a Whole Lotta Love Supreme
through Parliament/Funkadelic soul squeezes,
Sam Cooke lullabies
and Otis Redding kisses
until you and I
are finally
Freebirds.

A.J. Huffman

This is What it Sounds Like

White wings whimper as they are released.
Church bells drown their sorrowful symphony,
punctuating what they already know
to be punctured. The bride,
a vision in white, holds an ocean
of violets in bloom. She is the picture of appropriate
ignorance, smiling oblivious at her newly acquired mate.
She does not notice that his eyes and hands have
already been wandering. The anonymous blonde
creature of his secret affections sticks
to the shadows behind the very last pew.
The few guests who notice, find her tears touching.
They cannot hear the question echoing inside
her breaking heart: *How can you just leave me
standing, alone in a world that's so cold?*

*Inspired by *When Doves Cry* by Prince.

Shawn Aveningo

Forever 19

There is a place
where I am forever nineteen,
a place where I can tell my body how to move,
and it follows without creaking –

> *point your toes, arch your back,*
> *a little more, now reach with your fingertips*
> *to scratch the moon.*

There is a place
where I can sense the dancers
who came before me, their sweat
locked between coats of varnish.
I glide my palms across the cool
smooth surface, legs straddled
stretching, reaching closer
to myself in the studio mirror.

There is a place
where a torn day-glo sweatshirt
dripping off my shoulder,
is the preferred uniform of the day,
along with flesh-tone fishnets
and capezios so broken-in, I can see the outline
of salt-stained toes in the worn leather.

There is a place
where the artist formally known as Prince
sings *Baby I'm A Star,* and with one sip
of metallic, lukewarm water
from the corner drinking fountain,
and another day of *pas de bourrée – jetté – plié,*
I believe
I really can be.

Sarah Key

Nipples Up

To the sky! says Ms. Manno my African
dance teacher. We will find your tribe, are
you Congo? she trills on tempo to me. No men,
we are greying Jewesses at the barre,
feet planted fingers skyward, mesdames
we ache to be tangled in the beat of history.
Our instructress taught by Dame Dunham
herself years ago crossed the emerald sea
to be torn from Montserrat's teat. Lava spilt
across nippled earth to erase the hum
of living dirt that birthed many a lilt.
What sacrifice! She saves our stories by drum
makes us bow salute the skin wave our hips
kiss the ground feel our ancestral lips.

Judith Kelly Quaempts

Piazzolla and Me

Tango playing in my ears
I stride sedately until I reach a path
obscured by overreaching trees. Then,
melting into music invisible as air,
I dance ... graceful as the morning breeze.

With a partner only I can see
I bend and sway, swoop and glide,
dip and twirl beneath the silent leaves.
Young again, my skin porcelain,
my neck so long and lissome
even swans must weep in envy.

I dance until the world intrudes.
A woman walking her little dog,
a park employee raking leaves.
Shape shifting, I transform again
into this aged façade. I smile,
say good morning as I bend
to pet the dog, the tango
only I can hear
fading like an interrupted dream.

Dudamel at Disney Hall

    Gustavo dances
    and shows some gum

    and the harpists s-t-r-u-m
    and the tympani Tum-Tum
    and the basses thrummm-thrummm

    while the trumpets TOOT
    and the French horns HOOT
    and the flutists ... flute

    and the celeste tinkle-tinkles
    the glockenspiel tinkle-tenkles
    the xylophone tinkle-tankles
    and the marimba tinkle-tonkles

    and the gong goes
    WHUMMMMMMmmmmmmmmmmmmmm

    Let's get up and dance with Gustavo!
    and show our gums and
    creak our hips and
    crack our knees and
    pop our ankles and
    whirl and twist and thump and spin
    like ancient angels on the head of a pin —

    Or we could sit and just hold hands
    and listen to the joyous din!

Jacqueline Jules

Falling in Love

Ed Sullivan said no cameras below the waist.
That Elvis Presley got the girls "All Shook Up"
and Sullivan wouldn't "Surrender"
to hips swiveling with the beat.

Elvis wasn't born "In the Ghetto,"
but he knew poverty in Mississippi and Tennessee,
and how it felt to live in "Heartbreak Hotel."
Colonel Parker propelled him to "Fame and Fortune"
and overnight, he had "Too Much"
at the price of being "A Puppet on a String."

His fans loved him tender in more than 30 films,
where he rocked in a jailhouse,
sang on the beach of "Blue Hawaii," and found
"A Hard Headed Woman" in New Orleans.

But it was his voice,
rocking us "Way Down" and
back up to "The Promised Land"
that made us call him King. It poured
from the stage like a "Kentucky Rain"
drenching us in a sound
that made us raise our arms and proclaim:
we "Can't Help Falling in Love."

Christopher Luna

King of What? King of Who?

there is nothing regal about
the way Elvis would go crosseyed
every time he did something cute
in one of his "movies"
nothing rocking
about the minstrel show
spoon fed to young white girls
to protect them from Chuck Berry
Muddy Waters, and Little Richard

and if he truly loved the music he
aped, watered down, and emasculated
that pained look of embarrassment
he wears onscreen
must reflect his awareness
that he would forever remain second rate
a pale imitation

Christopher Scribner

Blues, 1961

He's Peter Chatman, Buddy-Boy, but
goes by Memphis Slim.
Tall lean commanding presence,
boasts a mellow baritone of burnished
brass, angry mournful
resonations, slaps
of racism give
the rhythm.
Sings the Mississippi water tastes
like turpentine.
Sings of Mother Earth's relentless
beckon, everybody equal
in the end.
Piano touch skitters,
impassioned driving pulsing
of the upper keys, black
ones mostly, propelling the whole of it —
humiliation, pain, atrocities,
indignities of all sizes,
experiences of this large
dark man treated small.
Filtered through his spirit
to his fingertips to the ivories,
before the time of keys
no longer made of ivory —
elephants afforded more concern
and protection than he received.
Hell and hardships would not cow
him, but fuel the music. The skitter,
energy born of hard times,
defiant insistent vitality coursing
through his spirit to his fingertips
to the ivories,

then through me, pounding
a path of pain and passion, my white
skin turning darker with a bruise
throbbing still
after the music ends.

 Julene Tripp Weaver

In Our Strange Home

Hip Hop Nation
        heeds
                the plea to respond
Horn blast
      wake-up call
           to pick up the slack

Some Hip Hop shot
          going to rock
                light fires
Set cities aflame
        with Harlem Renaissance
                where riots used to glow

Hendrix
      crossed
           the color-line
Bright
      bold
           peacock shine

Something lost in my
            teeny-bopper holler
                blind screech
                      We want the Monkees
                      We want the Monkees

What is it
      in this strange home
             we fascinate on
Under-the-wire
      weather storms

Reign
        in our fear-swept

              white-heavy nation

Word-by-word
          crows begin to sing

Their voices join
          heaven's rock & roll band
                play perfect pitch

Music floats the sky
        black birds cheer us on
              want us to sing along
But can
        we hear their music call
And when
        will we respond

Trained mutts sit at our heels
        Hip Hop Nation
                picks up the bone
Runs it over the start line,
        says go, in less than words
                but more than words can say

It is time,
        renaissance revival time

People of all colors
        must sing loud
                our aggressive needs proud

A deep moan low in the throat
                song before words

Hip Hop Nation
            delivers

In my fifties now
            able to scream,
                      Hendrix, Hendrix, Hendrix
I want his voice,
            his elder voice
                      burned out too soon
In our strange home
            where he landed below the color-line

                              where we all
                                          die

 Lennart Lundh

Little Boxes

      Grandpa, he asks, is that punk rock?
          No, child, I reply, *those are the Kinks;*
        they were British Invasion.
      Oh? Online, it says they were protopunk.
         Is that, I joke, like nouveau-retro-rockabilly?

He doesn't get it. Nor do I.
There's something cosmic-not-so-funny here,
though I'm sure the gods are laughing.
Where does it come from, this urge to
segregate, classify, mystify?
Blacks at that fountain, Jews at that part of the Wall,
Cubs versus Sox, and that side of the street is Canada?
And just how the hell did Question Mark and the Mysterians
beget Sid Vicious and the Velvet Underground?

Bill Cushing

"Music isn't about standing still and being safe."
~ *Miles Davis (1926–1991)*

    listen

    two weeks after you died
    a quarter-million thronged
    by the St. Johns River
    to hear the music you had spawned
    hoping to see you
    but
    even in death
    you never looked back

    they were all there
           Hannibal   Bird
           Chick   Jo-Jo
           Red   Jaco
           Bean   Dizzy
           my favorite   Freddie Freeloader

    isolated
    you
    were a beacon
           a flagship for messages
                of the heart

    back to the crowd   unbowed
    that proud dance-walk
    announced by muted horn
    that spoke
    and broke
    through all the bull
    and told us about a place

Miles

ahead of everyone else
you spent a lifetime
        thinking for yourself
        speaking to every generation
playing it all:
        jazz   blues
        funk   rock
        fusion
categories took
a backseat
to creativity
        and rhythm

        space

        and feeling
                spirit

I remember fourth grade
picking up a horn
then laying it down
rock and roll was my world
what did I know

seven years later I heard

it was in the Garden
where you brought me back
to music

I walked all the way home

Miles

from that train station

my head pounding with sounds
frantic-fast as the subway
I spent the night on
          those African rhythms
          you used decades
          before anyone else
          even thought to
filling my head
letting me know
I'd have it all down cold
if I could walk
as cool as the notes you heard
          coming from

Miles

you had that thing
          that style
that spark that was
a blue flame
          jumping
          off a gas stove
igniting everything   everywhere
touching the genetic
resonant
frequency
in all

Akua Lezli Hope

Betty Carter

Filled with horn riffs
flight of the swift
loaded with chirp
and twitter   deep tweets
a blur of buttery kisses
a flurry of sonic blows
wind's slow praline voice
when it swoops down to caress
your face, sustains, enfolds
and fingers your hair

Her voice is hillock

Her voice is backyard tree
between brownstones
and gold shoes on Lexington Avenue
figured bass, luscious lute
post modern still ever new

She mothers it — a deepening
crafts it — an excision
in the flight, in the landing
her arching tone, a precision

The rolling ball unravels
a strip of bright sky
you journey on attenuated sighs
what happens after two strings are plucked
vibration's purple motion hums
and you are struck
by what enters through your ears
and unfolds to gently rearrange your heart

Helen Kerner

Word Jazz

Oh the jazz of words,
like hip hop,   skip a rock
like hearing a foreign language,
          but we're fluent, intuit
every ripe, rich sound, around
          lush and flush such a rush,
the music lifting, drifting
in lazy hazy daisy current,
or rapids driving   diving from on high,
     words sing and call as they fall
and souls take them all,   begin
          to dance, prance, jump up and down
                over ground,
the floor under our feet, sweet,
     whether two-step or be-bop
          doo-wop, boogie, waltz or twist,
                don't resist
it all unwinds us,   aligns us
to listen again and again,
to find and bend,   then sing aloud
     proud, by rote to float above the rest
and test   *word jazz*   the giggles
and shouts
          freak us out
     but we can't stop our shoulders
from swaying,   hips pop forayin'
     the joy, just sayin', of the day
riper than a cornucopia of spilled fruit.
     We are astute and root for more,
the notes, the words,   the rhythm
     the blues, from mutter to stutter
all chants repeated tweeted
sacred rune of tribal law

                        that's all we need
    to thrive & survive
            just keep the word jazz
    turned up high   and try
    to keep it   playin'

Janet Cloyd

Dispatches from the Microphone & Microphone Stand Perspective

Sing into me.
Pour your melodies into my silver neck.

Hold on to me tight.
Place your right foot on the very bottom of me
for your grounding and safekeeping.

I am the witness to the truth drizzling out of your
songstress riddled throat.
I am the mouthpiece for your music surrendered.

Believe in the first note you sing.
Believe in the last note you sing.
You will make believers out of all who will journey into your song.

Dig deep   mine the diamonds of rhythm, base and treble.
Unearth   songs sung by those who were midwives
to the music birthed in the ears of today.

Whenever you become
nervous
or
unsure
or
unraveled
or
unappreciated

reach down and caress my silver neck.
It will always be cool to the touch.

# Oreł Protopopescu

Listening to *My Favorite Things*
From *The Best of John Coltrane*

I never liked this silly song
before I got hooked on the way
brushes whisper to the drum heads
as Trane dips and slides over the melody,
teasing me with his horn,
drawing me along the edge
of the abyss where his star pulses.

His notes appear and disappear
like those slim, beautiful boys
who played basketball in torn Keds
and leaned against the rough brick walls
of the projects until their dark skins
were scraped with comet trails.

Some lost half-lives to heroin,
to prison, to grief held back
until they burst the way
Coltrane explodes in my ears,
horn chattering like a crazed parrot,
shredding the melody and taking it
up where he wails and climbs.

When he drags it back,
that annoying tune is a snake charmer's dirge,
slower, sadder, older, wiser,
like my old friends,
sometime boys who shot for the stars
and fell, leaving their music in my head.

So I cry when,
after taking me so far,

after thirteen eternal minutes,
Trane knots a perfect loop
of pure round sound,
then strangles it.

Mark Kerstetter

Moonwalker

Long before our season of falling icons,
in a sky of purple rain we'd prepped to mourn
the passing of the Thin White Duke and cry, *Never!*
In fact we'd sidled up to goodbye for years,
some in silence, some with jeers.
Goodbye to the boy forever escaping
the cares of accountants' careers,
the tabloids gaping and nose jobs botched,
to the dangling baby caught
by a single sequined glove
while German tourists watched in shock
and others for tastier fare than *Thriller*
sought answers for a boy, alone,
in Neverland.

Painkillers.
Million dollar-spending sprees
were not enough to recover the loss.

Never can say —
from Neverland to Bahrain,
from Megalomania Awards to Soul Train,
to the creature not meant for this world
and the moonwalker down below —
maybe a half century here
is just enough to know
the mirror in the man.

Today they unearthed a flute
more than thirty thousand years buried.
It belonged to a boy
just like you.

Dan Raphael

If Jimi Hadn't Died So Young

In this world Jimi Hendrix didn't die at 27
but kept advancing his prowess on the guitar,
playing two at once, multiple strings. like Chaplin
he could do anything he did
backwards as well, and sometimes would start a song in the middle
and go 4 or 6 different ways from there,
ensphering himself and listeners
in shifting laminae of sound.

At a show in Philly most of the audience blacked out,
several suffered "stroke-like symptoms," two disappeared.
With a lawsuit filed by a victim, the government seized Jimi's guitars,
the Pentagon volunteering to study the evidence.
More guitars were built.
More people plugged into Hendrix
and played guitars several hours a day.
No one knew if Jimi was in jail, hiding, or if his playing
had opened new dimensions in vibratory time.

Are we still on the same world we started on?
What chords could I make with 9 strings and six fingers?
Reports of others disappearing while Hendrix played, with the feds
suppressing the total.
On March 1st
a 10 meter tall transparent creature emitting guitar-like sounds
shattered a 2 kilometer stretch of the great wall of China,
then vanished in a rancid fog.
In paranoid anticipation, guitarists cleared music store shelves
of strings.

The sun rose with ear splitting feedback surrendering
to an arpeggio of random vertebra,
nerve triggers ranging from St. Vitus to waltz, many unable to drive

coz theyre feet wouldn't stay still. Radios were ignored, no ear buds
could keep out the panoply of music, bodies finding new limbs,
my feet trading myccorhizally while my suddenly tendriled hair
embraces the pollen filled sky, billions of microscopic notes
ready to bloom into life-expanding solos,
some neighborhoods so thick with music
you need neither amplifier or guitar, you and the air
collaborating symphonies
to take us where we never could be.

David Belmont

Train Sounds

Philip Glass says his music sounds like New York City
He tells a story about a long train ride
and hearing the click clack repetition of the rails

On some days when I was in high school
I'd drop some acid
and ride the elevated train out to Flushing

I thought it sounded like Hendrix

Now I realize that it probably sounded like Hendrix
to Jimi too

Linda Goulden

Session Man

He's a steel-string sizzle in a slider-bind
a rope bass fumble with a cat-gut whine
a thumb and finger picking at a flat wishbone
a minor bellow, a major drone
a dumb drum rolling up the underground
the semaphore of siren sound
one hammer-on behind the gong
a blue note swinging in a slip-knot song.

Josh Gaines

Sax Axis

Corner of
rooftop and jazz,
top of sound waves
the sweet of fresh baked,
earth of waking coffee pots
alarms foot tapping symbol crash
smack clack and flail,
the floor already
warming with vibration.

Deciding what makes
the world go round,
in the building where music lives,
everyone who wants to be
anyone worth remembering
chats up old timers
for trade secrets:
      How he held the thing wrong
      Even then wouldn't touch the stuff
      Covered his lips in Carmex
They pile on the how in the hell mystique,
      Never owned a clock in his life and
      never late for a gig.
      Dizzy woke to imagination,
      a reveille of *Do-Be-Dat!*
      squeaking through his ears
      like Beethoven's brass
      deaf to the sounds
      of the day.

Today's movement
plays off traffic horns' jam,
trash can steel's crashing battle,

the muted-piano pigeon coos
on a roof
with the band
who plays the sunrise
to the drowned by endless incandescence
halogen fluorescence
star sparse sky,
the hopes of immigrant shoulders
the promises of free flow
on a breeze of asphalt
and cherry blossoms.

A blackbird remains antenna perched
before a cloudless summer.
Before a trumpet no longer on a march,
time saunters.

By night, time and trombones slide
with bands' howling midnight saxes,
a nightly practice of
feet pressing earth to music's entrancing.
The world spins on its axis
because we keep dancing.

Marj Hahne

Center, Fleeing

It's Dave Matthews' milky tenor
on the stereo that gets me
out of my chair, abandoning
the computer at the kitchen table,
to slip impatient hips into a hula
hoop filled with dried legumes spinning
confetti sound around the room
— lentils, soybeans, split peas? —
but here's the real question:
Would I rather be dancing with you
in the cool dark of your living room,
doing something like the bump and
grind, more body on air, less bone
against bone?   Dave's voice goes high
then low then high like no one's, his
and Tim's guitars always keeping up, two
tides becoming one wave that has my hips
moving like honey on a spoon, the hoop
defying the gravity of this heart-heavy
world, a physics imperceptible but still
centrifugal: *centrum* + *fugere* — two
forces, one centering, one fleeing
like the moon trying to leave the earth.

Peter Goodwin

On First Hearing The Voice Of Joan Baez

Just arrived on these shores
taking classes at college
thinking America merely
a bigger and brasher
version of England
still wearing a tie and jacket
leather shoes polished
a polished English accent
indifferent to matters
of race and justice.
A new friend, whose conversation
was erratic, brilliant and brash
who always needed a shave
suggested going to a conference
a conference on civil rights
so I followed.
We picked up others
in the old part of town
in a worn out building
with wooden floors
high ceilings, cracked plaster
and a beautiful sound
floating through the air
clean, clear, angelic
penetrating into my soul.
What is that? I ask
standing still, in a trance
until then indifferent to music
bored with song
now listening to a song
sung by an angel
that wrapped itself around me
transforming me

awakening a part of me
that had been dormant
and though we all
bundled into a car
it was her voice
that led me across town
to the Negro College
into a crowd where
my pale skin marked me
listening to speeches
filled with the rhythm
of the African American Church
talking of injustice, of oppression
oppression by white people
people like myself
voices of passion
voices of humor
voices demanding change
voices that would create change
and that evening, that weekend
I became an American
involved in a great American struggle
and that voice
that pure American voice
helped take me
on that great American journey.

Jane Yolen

Singing with Pete

> *"The words of the songs had all the meat of life in them."*
> *~ Pete Seeger*

Singing along with Pete was like a full course meal,
and you didn't have to dress fancy or use your best manners.
Just open up your mouth and give it a holler.
You could use your fingers, too, snapping them,
playing the spoons, hitting the sides of your thighs
with open hands, like they were castanets, he didn't care.
It was all music to him, body music, the meat of life.

He invited us all to the table, union man and boss together,
summer patriot and winter soldier plus a good old helping
of conscientious objector besides. Everyone got some.
It wasn't just metaphor, you know. It was the real deal.
You never left his concerts hungry, but carried those tunes
home in a tote sack, to snack on all the rest of your life.

Donna Barkman

Michigan Womyn's Music Festival
Otherwise Known As Mich

Cars and charter buses pant in the brash sun
waiting for the gates to open
Rainbow flags and women's equality banners flap from antennas
and open windows
                We'll arrive late, lost as usual
Butch-Alice asks a roadside vendor *Seen any women who look like me?*
    He blusters *Ohhh, yes, and more so!*
Greeters call: *Any Festie Virgins here?* No first-timers with us
Everyone signs up for a work shift, four hours required, with more
gratefully accepted:
    child-care workers, Porta-Jane cleaners, cooks and servers,
        guards: *Man-on-the land!* when deliveries arrive
Topless or bottomless — some of us duck; others proudly present

Tents bloom in fields of four-foot-high ferns,
I see Holly. Isn't that Chris? Old-timers know *The Changer and the Changed*,
        Hay Una Mujer Deseparacida
We sing our versions, anticipating theirs
Open-air showers not cooling enough
                the storm arrives!
We strip what's left and roll in the flood, shrieking, throwing mud balls
Jump on the tractor-shuttle, quick, beat the lines
Veggie dinner's ready
            then it's the music
Techies climb scaffolding
                musicians tune up

We carelessly gather
arrange blankets
beach chairs
near lovers
ex-lovers
partners
and friends

David Jibson

Tracy Chapman

Give Me One Reason presents a real challenge.
What reason, if I'm allowed only one,
would be good enough?

My granddaughter, who idolizes Ariana Grande,
asks me who is singing. I tell her.
Then she wants to know if it's a man or a woman
because she can't tell from the voice or the name.

I listen to Tracy strum and pick her way
through the sharps and sevenths
of her perfect blues progression.

I answer back to her,
"Give me one reason why it matters."

Jeffrey H. MacLachlan

Hit Song

You claim to lock your ears to my knocking but you drum the even rhythm. I just demand three minutes to cartwheel through your spine and then you can have your limbs back. But I'm bringing the big top. I'm bringing snake charmers and fire dancers and mimes. Your wife's dinner conversations are my verses and her pillow talk is my hook. Infect her ear with my melody and the spell will finally pop.

Shahé Mankerian

At Marilyn's Backstreet Disco

I don't remember the glitter on the popcorn ceiling
or the neon mustache on the sound proofed walls.

We drooped on balcony rails and drooled over girls
draped in fishnet tops. Even the Teddy Boys

wanted birthmarks above their lips like Madonna.
Lovers reclined on the flabby couch; wallets went

missing between velvet cushions. The bathroom
coughed; girls with fingerless gloves crammed

on the dance floor. The deejay's pompadour hair
brushed against the chandelier full of cobwebs.

Once, I found a shoulder pad near the emergency exit.
When I used it to dab my sweat, it reeked of Drakkar Noir.

This Ain't No Disco

"Stands for Country, Blue Grass and Blues,"
Fred informed me, his disdain
evident in his dismissive tone.
An old folk music fan
who'd even had problems adjusting
when Dylan went electric at Newport,
Fred couldn't abide our younger friends
when they returned to Boston
from a weekend in New York,
full of tales of seeing the Ramones,
first-naming Joey and Johnny and Dee Dee,
falling all over themselves declaring
how much they wanted to fuck Debbie Harry,
after getting into the club for a Blondie show,
how close they came to touching her.

"They won't last," Fred pronounced, confident
in his prediction. "This time next year
nobody'll remember CBGB either."

Carolyn Martin

How to Write a Great Country Song

three chords and the truth and throw in
half-dozen sweaty beers, a red guitar,
a slow-talking gal who sets you dreamin'
how her breasts would feel if she was willin'
and you were so inclined when your fingers
find the chords and you work your rhymes for curves
and heft, beauty marks, and nipples risin'
long before her clothes slide off and how
you'll rope her in with strings of half-slant lines
that make it clear tonight is all about
a few more swigs and sex on worn-out sheets
with nothin' more in mind but then she ups
and leaves with *it was mighty nice* and how
she might have stayed but she won't pay the price
for bein' one more one-night nights you fret
about in three-chord sets and so you trash
your rhymes and case your silenced red guitar
and hear a country song struttin' out the door.

Susana H. Case

Karaoke Bar, Brooklyn

The mountain mama takes her turn
on the stage, belts out
Take Me Home, Country Roads
with a nasal Appalachian upland
twang, puts her whole skinny body
into the moan of *West Virginia*,
like the songwriter, who'd never
been to West Virginia
when he penned the plaintive
words of love. No matter she's not
from West Virginia. No matter
she can't carry a tune.
The last weekend of summer,
not dark enough yet for fireworks,
she is already ignited, raises her arms
in praise. Home is the poem,
she's telling us, home is the prayer,
home is the winding road.

Lynn M. Knapp

La Música

Disorderly optimism and muscular vitality
echo through the alleys, *en las callejones.*

I want to find the music,
be part of that bursting, riotous life,
leave my old life behind.

I want black eyes, brown skin,
a lilting language on my lips
and *alegria* in my heart.

I want to ride the crest of that wave
swamping everything before it,
claiming my old country and making it new.

But I cannot go with them.
I am the other, *la gabacha,* the white girl in the big gray house
with one foot in the old world and one in the new.

Bill Frayer

The Singing Señoras of Guayabidos

They have come again
to the same old beach hotel.
Old sisters. They sit together
in white plastic chairs and laugh
as they sip their piña coladas.

Some cannot hear;
some cannot walk alone,
but they return to love
and fetch food for one another,
and bask in their smiles.

Every night they sit
in their beach dresses
red, yellow, lavender, blue,
and tap their flip flops
and they sing.
They know all the words
to the Mexican songs
national songs
tragic songs
childhood songs.

And they enchant us all
as they sing and they cry
as they sip
their piña coladas
and hold one another
in their hearts
for one more night.

Brad G. Garber

Cajun Bluegrass

It's all about happy music, quick music
the beat just ahead of the heart but behind
the mind, the stuff that makes muscles
move unconsciously like sex, the difference
between water over stones and a meadowlark
get the banjo, get the drums, get the mandolin
raining hot notes, bare feet, open palms
dust rising, dust flying, dust and laughter
step step, kick … step step kick … twirl
spinning away, spinning in, spinning
the sounds of the world in our bodies
not Senegal, not Spain, not Ireland
but cellular, subcellular, sub-brainwave
grab, hold, slide, arch, turn, hop, jump
like something at the end of electric
at the end of a volcano's blast, at the end
of strings of beads and open breasts
the siren sounds of percolating brooks
undercurrent of escaping sound, animals
beginning to sense what they really are.

Ellaraine Lockie

Song from the Other Side

Arlo knew the secret
long before scientists conceived cloning
He discovered it in the guitar strums
and famous folk lyrics from his father
Toured the country with reincarnate rituals
Mouth-to-mouth resuscitation songs
that released Woody from his soundproofed box

But did he know how many
other resurrections he wrought
How the first bars of *Goodnight Irene*
could recall forgotten renditions from other fathers
Like one who sat singing beside a bed
banishing nightmares and cooling fevers
With such nostalgia that the daughter
thought Irene might have been her mother

Did Arlo know how his lyrics released
those moments long held in ransom
Before breasts budded
and fevers that became adolescent endemic
refused to be soothed by a song
And there was no antidote
for the parental paralysis that followed

Frozen feelings that
endured the test of time
While the daughter slipped
on them in icy dreams
Until songs from the dead
melted early memories
That dribbled out and down
her cheeks in a concert hall

Douglas Spangle

Father-Daughter Act

He's gone gray, thinning stray
wisps dancing on his dome —
sports well-worn flannel plaid,
his hands held over the strings
and sound-hole of an aging acoustic,

talking to another guy of a similar
vintage in ponytail and denim.
She's a lean blonde, silent, gawky
and sixteen, in the demi-mode remains
of an oversized leisure suit,

her new and polished Stratocaster
also mute and resting in her lap.
Dutiful Daughter, says her posture,
but her light-lashed eyes occupy
a space that emanates music.

I'd heard a few runs from those
fingers that were made for fretplay
before I'd stepped over the curb
catty-corner across the intersection
at my peril against the light.

His guitar case is an empty palm between them.
I fold up a bill really tiny, aim,
toss, and for once in my life,
hit the mark with ease. He
doesn't notice, still talking; she

looks right at me, music
worth a million bills in her eyes.
Her lips smile in gratitude, proud
slender fingers still at rest
on her lovely instrument.

Tiffany M. Burba

Music Heals

I've heard music can heal
so powerful it changed
thirty years of pain in one night

I watch my dad and brother
stand side by side on
a wooden stage, faces smiling
they sing The Jamaica Farewell

I hear dad express his dream
to be on stage with his youngest son
after all the missed concerts,
football games and let downs
those disappointments float like bubbles
up from the ground, one by one
where they burst open
and vanish

Kathleen Corcoran

The Final Message in a Song

At seventy he practiced playing the piano
making up for childhood grumbles while shuffling
to Auntie May's for lessons when he'd rather
be outside playing with neighborhood friends.

He played "Danny Boy," and I heard chords grow
stronger even as his heart grew weaker,
and his fingers more bent with arthritis.
I heard his thoughts of glens and mountain-sides,

his Ireland which he left for me. I heard
our lives together, sun and shadow merging.
In his last wishes he asked that "Danny Boy"
be sung, and at the final service the song

brought comfort, telling me he'll sleep in peace,
leaving me with final words – "I love you so."

Kenneth Salzmann

What But the Music

Maybe graying women and balding men are gathering
right now in every improbable town that hugs
a two-digit highway pointing vaguely toward America.

Maybe it's turning out we are unremarkable, after all —
unique and universal, just like all the rest.

Maybe it's nothing but the same comfortable crawl
every generation makes toward first things and well-worn
memories, when they start to notice the obituaries
are piling up higher than anyone ever thought they could.

Or maybe it is the music, after all.

What but the music might have orchestrated
forgotten revolutions and unforgettable kisses?
What but the music underscored every presumed
triumph and defeat, drew us into church basements
and into cheap apartments in bad neighborhoods,
ripped down walls, egged us on, played us out?

But maybe a soundtrack laid down decades ago
can permeate our souls and chart our lives
until one day we begin to see — long after we've
stopped looking — that astonishing rhythms
really did change the world.

What but the music might have bound us then?
What but the music might bind us again?

Acknowledgments

We gratefully acknowledge the following publications in which these poems first appeared:

"A Familiar Song" by Ada Jill Schneider was previously published in *This Once-Only World* (PearTree Press, Fall River, MA, 2015).

"Song of the Katabatic Wind" by Jennifer Fenn first appeared in author's self-published chapbook, *Song of the Katabatic Wind* (Fresno, CA, October 2015).

"Theory of Choir" by Annette L. Grunseth was previously published in *An Ariel Anthology* (Washburn, WI, December 2015).

"Let it Be" by Connie Post was first published in *Bloodroot* (2011).

"Abbey Road" by Nancy Haskett was first published online in *Homestead Review* (Fall 2015) and in *The Gathering 13* (The Ina Coolbrith Circle, 2015).

"There Are More Verses to This Song" by Cynthia Linville was first published in *WTF #13* (Sacramento, CA 2012).

"Forever 19" by Shawn Aveningo also appears in the Delaware Poetry Review's special edition, *This Thing Called Life: Poetry Inspired by the Music and Spirit of Prince* (2016).

"Little Boxes" by Lennart Lundh first appeared in *National Poetry Month Anthology* 2013 (Writing Knights Press).

"Music isn't about standing still and being safe" by Bill Cushing was originally published in *Stories of Music*, Volume 1.

"Listening to *My Favorite Things* from *The Best of John Coltrane*" by Orel Protopopescu was previously published as the first prize winner in *Oberon Poetry Magazine* (2010).

"Song from the Other Side" by Ellaraine Lockie was first published in *Jukebox Junction* USA Special Edition.

"What But the Music" by Kenneth Salzmann was previously published in *Stories of Music*, Volume 1.

Contributors

A.J. Huffman's poetry, fiction, haiku, and photography have appeared in hundreds of national and international journals. She is also the founding editor of Kind of a Hurricane Press. <kindofahurricanepress.com>

Ada Jill Schneider's latest volume of poetry is *This Once-Only World* (PearTree Press 2015). She directs "The Pleasure of Poetry" at the Somerset Public Library in Massachusetts. Winner of the National Galway Kinnell Poetry Prize, Ada started writing poetry at the age of 53, when she thought she was old. <adajillschneider.com>

Akua Lezli Hope is a creator who uses sound, words, fiber, glass, metal, and wire to create poems, patterns, stories, music, ornaments, wearables, jewelry, adornments and peace whenever possible. Her manuscript, *Them Gone*, won Red Paint Hill Publishing's Editor's Prize and will be published in 2016. <akualezlihope.com>

Alan Catlin has been publishing since the 70's. His credits range from the well-respected, to the mundane, to the totally obscure. His most recent book is *American Odyssey* from Future Cycle. He is poetry editor of misfitmagazine.net <thecatlins@msn.com>

Amy Miller's poetry has appeared in *Nimrod, Rattle, ZYZZYVA,* and other journals. Her first job, at age 17, was as a receptionist for a magazine that featured bombers and jet fighters on the cover. She happily left the defense industry for the music business and still works in publishing. <writers-island.blogspot.com>

Anne Harding Woodworth's fifth book of poetry is *Unattached Male* (2014, Poetry Salzburg). Her fourth chapbook, *The Last Gun*, appeared in April 2016. Harding Woodworth sits on the Poetry Board of the Folger Shakespeare Library, Washington DC, where she lives and sings alto with the City Choir of Washington. <annewoodworth@yahoo.com>

Anne Whitehouse is the author of six poetry collections, most recently *Meteor Shower* from Dos Madres Press. Her novel, *Fall Love*, is translated into Spanish as *Amigos y amantes*. Recent honors include the 2016 *Songs of Eretz* poetry prize, 2016 *RhymeOn!* poetry prize, and the Common Good Books' poems of gratitude contest. She is from Birmingham, Alabama, and lives in New York City. <annewhitehouse.com>

Annette L. Grunseth, Green Bay, WI, a graduate of University of Wisconsin, Madison, is a retired Marketing/Public Relations professional. Her poems have appeared in *Wisconsin Academy Review, Midwest Prairie Review, SOUNDINGS: Door County in Poetry* and other anthologies. Her passions include singing in a really great choir and writing poetry. <annettegrunseth@gmail.com>

Bill Cushing lived in numerous states, the Virgin Islands, and Puerto Rico before returning to school. He moved to California after earning an MFA in writing from Goddard College and teaches college English in the Los Angeles area. His current project, "Notes and Letters," mixes original music with poetry. <piscespoet@yahoo.com>

Bill Frayer is a retired community college professor who splits his time between Maine and Mexico. He's published four volumes of poetry, and has been writing a monthly column for the English-language monthy, *El Ojo del Lago*, in Mexico, for the past nine years. He enjoys playing acoustic blues guitar. <billfrayer@gmail.com>

Brad G. Garber lives, writes and runs around naked in the Great Northwest. He fills his home with art, music, photography, plants, rocks, bones, books, good cookin' and love. He has published poetry, art, photos, essays and articles in many quality publications. 2013 Pushcart Prize nominee. <bggarber@yahoo.com>

Carol Taylor Was is the Poetry Editor for *The MacGuffin*. Her work appeared in *The Gettysburg Review* and the *Southern Review*. Her passions are poetry, fossil hunting, and all creatures in the natural world. She's prepared bones in a fossil lab for a Triceratops, and a 250 million-year-old Nebraskan turtle.

Carolyn Dahl, Grand Prize winner of the 2015 Public Poetry/MFAH ekphrastic competition, has been published in 25 anthologies and in *Copper Nickel, Camas, & Hawaii Review*. A former singer, she played Maria (West Side Story) happily until another actor knocked off her black wig, revealing she was really blonde. <carolyndahlstudio.com>

Carolyn Martin cannot carry a tune or play an instrument, so she uses poetry to create music. Her poems and book reviews have appeared throughout the US and UK, and her second collection, *The Way a Woman Knows*, was released by The Poetry Box in 2015. <portlandpoet@gmail.com>

Charles Rammelkamp is Prose Editor for BrickHouse Books in Baltimore, where he lives, and edits *The Potomac*, an online literary journal. His latest book is a collection of poems called *Mata Hari: Eye of the Day* (Apprentice House, Loyola University). *American Zeitgeist*, is forthcoming from Apprentice House next year. <annamelkamp@verizon.net>

Clark County, WA Poet Laureate **Christopher Luna** has been collaborating with musicians for a quarter century. He has an MFA from the Jack Kerouac School of Disembodied Poetics, where he performed his poetry with musicians including Totter, Jason Levis, Rob Ewing, Tyler Burba, and Steven Taylor. <printedmattervancouver.com>

Christopher Scribner strives to be the best poet amongst Clinical Psychologists and the best psychologist amongst poets. He completed his MFA at Lindenwood University and has pieces published or forthcoming in *Euphony, The Quarterday Review, Rat's Ass Review,* and some other places. <insight7@sbcglobal.net>

Claudia F. Savage is one-half of the music-poetry duo *Thick in the Throat, Honey*. She's been published in *Water-Stone Review, Denver Quarterly,* and *Columbia Journal*. Her first book, *Bruising Continents* (Spuyten Duyvil) arrives Spring 2017. Besides poet, she's been a roller-skating waitress, lounge pianist, and chef. <claudiafsavage.com>.

Colette Tennant has played piano since she was five and loves to play jazz piano in particular. She writes music for kids and for adults. Her second book of poetry, *Eden and After*, was published by Tebot Bach, July 2015. Ask her to accompany your poetry reading. <ctennant@corban.edu>

Connie Post served as Poet Laureate of Livermore, California (2005-2009). Her work has appeared in *Calyx, Cold Mountain Review, Crab Creek Review, Comstock Review, Slipstream, Spoon River Poetry Review*. Her first full length manuscript *Floodwater*, released in 2014 by Glass Lyre Press, was awarded the Lyrebird Book Award. <poetrypost.com>

Cynthia Linville's two poetry collections, *The Lost Thing* and *Out of Reach*, are available from Cold River Press. Linville has served as Managing Editor of *Convergence* (convergence-journal.com) since 2008. A music aficionado with a theater background, she occasionally appears with musicians and with the group Poetica Erotica.

For a couple decades, **Dan Raphael**'s been active in the Northwest as poet, performer, editor and reading host. *Everyone in This Movie Gets Paid*, his 18th book, came out in June form Last Word Press. <raphael@aracnet.com>

David Belmont is a mixed media artist and community organizer living in New York City. An indie musician before the phrase was coined, he has produced over 30 albums since 1975. David's work has appeared *The Poeming Pigeon* and *Wildflower Muse*. He is currently co-music director of the Castillo Theatre. <davidbelmontwriter.wordpress.com>

David Jibson lives in Ann Arbor, Michigan where he is an associate editor of *Third Wednesday*, a literary arts journal, a member of The Crazy Wisdom Poetry Circle and The Poetry Society of Michigan. He is retired from a career in social work, most recently with a hospice agency. <thirdwednesday.org>

Deborah Meltvedt is a writer and teacher in Sacramento who wishes she could sing but at least enjoys writing about songs in her life. <deborahjean7@comcast.net>

A Pushcart Prize nominee **Diana Cole**'s poems have appeared in numerous journals including *Slipstream, Poetry East,* and *The Main Street Rag*. She is a member of the Ocean State Poets in Rhode Island whose mission is to encourage the sharing of poetry and to help others find their own voices. <dianacole@fullchannel.net>

Diane Elayne Dees' poems have been published in many journals and anthologies. Diane, who is a psychotherapist in Louisiana, also publishes *Women Who Serve*, a blog that covers women's professional tennis worldwide. <womenwhoserve.blogspot.com>

Born into a family of Oshkosh Wisconsin actors, **Donna Barkman** started performing in kindergarten. Her solo play, *Hand-Me-Downs* was recently produced in NYC and Westchester. Her poetry has been published in *Chautauqua, Boston Literary Review, Adrienne Rich: a Tribute Anthology,* and others. She has enjoyed two writing residencies in Wyoming. She took piano lessons for some sixteen years, but now *Chopsticks* is a challenge. <barkman1@verizon.net>

Douglas Spangle grew up as a Park Service brat before moving overseas in his teens. He went to high school in Ankara, Turkey and college in Munich, Germany. He came to Portland in 1978, and was given the 2016 Stewart Holbrook Literary

Legacy Award. He also appears in *Poeming Pigeons*. <dspangle@earthlink.net>

Eileen McGurn is a teacher and a poet. She has published on the East Coast (where she's from) and the West Coast (where she lives). She works at the PACE Program for parenting students in North Clackamas where she teaches the most wonderful students in the world. <mcgurne@nclack.k12.or.us>

Ellaraine Lockie is a widely published and awarded author of poetry, nonfiction books and essays. Her eleventh chapbook, *Where the Meadowlark Sings*, won the 2014 Encircle Publication's Chapbook Contest. She teaches poetry workshops, is a frequent judge of poetry contests and serves as Poetry Editor for the lifestyles magazine, *Lilipoh*.

Gabriella Brand's writing has appeared in *Room Magazine, Cordite, StepAway, Switched on Gutenberg, Three Element Review, The Christian Science Monitor,* and several anthologies. She is a Pushcart Prize nominee. Gabriella divides her time between Connecticut, where she teaches foreign languages, and Quebec, where she canoes, hikes, daydreams and writes. <gabriellabrand.net>

Helen Kerner has been published in several Marin Poetry Center anthologies, *Stories With Grace, VoiceCatcher* and *The Poeming Pigeon: Poems about Food*. Her book of poetry and prose, *The Journey*, was published in 2007 about her 1993 bone marrow transplant for leukemia. <hlkerner@gmail.com>

Jack Maze was raised in Hollister, California, birthplace of the American biker. He's retired from the University of British Columbia in Vancouver, B. C., Canada. He has self-published three books of photos and poem with Dan Brooks and two books of poetry. He lives in Vancouver, B. C. <erry@shaw.ca>

Jacqueline Jules is the author of the poetry chapbooks *Field Trip to the Museum* and *Stronger Than Cleopatra*. Her poetry has appeared in 120 journals including *Broadkill River Review* and *Imitation Fruit*. She is also the author of 30 children's books. <jacquelinejules.com>

Jan Haag teaches English and journalism at Sacramento City College in Sacramento, California, and facilitates writing groups using the Amherst Writers & Artists method, which reminds people that their voices are worthy of the page. She is the author of a poetry collection, *Companion Spirit*. <janishaag.com>

Jane Miller's poetry has appeared in the *Summerset Review, Mojave River Review, cahoodaloodaling, Broadkill Review, Watershed Review, Midwest Quarterly* and *Crab Orchard Review* among others. She received a 2014 Individual Artist Fellowship in poetry from the Delaware Division of the Arts. She lives in Wilmington, DE. <jmmnos@verizon.net>

Jane Yolen, is the author of over 350 books, the first author honored with an Arts and Humanities Award by the New England Public Radio, and a New York Times bestselling writer. Her good coat was set on fire by one of her many awards. <janeyolen.com>

Janel Cloyd is a poet, fiction writer and essayist. She is Watering Hole Fellow, a member of Women's Writer's Poetry In Bloom. Cloyd is a mixed media artist with a concentration in collage, paper arts, fiber, text and images. Her work explores themes of womanhood, spirituality and the body aesthetic. <wordecho@hotmail.com>

Jeffrey H. MacLachlan has recent or forthcoming work in *New Ohio Review, Eleven Eleven, The William & Mary Review*, among others. He teaches literature at Georgia College & State University. He secretly wears WWE shirts below his suit jacket. He can be followed on Twitter @jeffmack.

Jennifer Fenn has written poetry since high school. Her poetry has appeared in fifteen different journals, both in print and online, including *Song of the San Joaquin, Brevities,* and *Time of Singing*. She self-published two chapbooks, *Blessings* and *Song of the Katabatic Wind*, as church fundraisers. <jenniferfenn75@gmail.com>

Jennifer Hambrick's poetry has been honored with a Pushcart Prize nomination, and her chapbook, *Unscathed* (NightBallet Press), was nominated for the Ohioana Book Award. She has won numerous awards for her work, which has been published in *Third Wednesday, Pudding Magazine, Eyedrum Periodically, A Narrow Fellow, World Haiku Review* (placewinner, Spring/Summer 2016 issue), and in many others. A classical musician and public radio broadcaster and web producer, Jennifer Hambrick lives in Columbus, Ohio. <jenniferhambrick.com>.

Joan Leotta has been writing on scraps of paper and performing on any stage since childhood. She is a journalist, story performer, picture book author and shell collector. Her poems can be found in previous issues of *The Poeming Pigeon,* online collections via Silver Birch Press and *Verse Virtual* among others. <joanleotta.wordpress.com>

JoAnn Anglin has been a member of Los Escritores del Nuevo Sol / Writers of the New Sun for 25 years. Her poems have been published in regional pubs and in some from farther afield. She doesn't have a particular style and says the poem seems to declare the style. <joannpen@icloud.com>

Josh Gaines ditched a promising military career to write books, run a profitless press, and build blanket forts with his daughter. He earned a writing MFA from SAIC, and is a 2016 Art Farm writer in residence. Find him at random readings, coffee shops, and bar stools around Portland, Oregon. <thoughtcrimepress.com>

Judith Arcana's two most recent chapbooks *Soon To Be A Major Motion Picture* (prose fiction) and *Here From Somewhere Else* (poetry) received small press awards, a doubleheader that makes her smile a lot and think good thoughts. <juditharcana.com>

Judith Barrington has published four poetry collections, including *The Conversation*. Her chapbook, *Lost Lands* won the Robin Becker Chapbook Award. She also won the Gregory O'Donoghue International Poetry Prize for 2013. She teaches in the USA and Europe and lives in Portland with her sweetie and their dog.

Judith Kelly Quaempts lives and writes in rural eastern Oregon. Her poetry appears, or is soon to appear, in *Persimmon Tree, Buddhist Poetry Review, Windfall: A Journal of Place,* and *Crafty Poet II: A Portable Workshop*. <jkquaempts@yahoo.com>

Judith Skillman's recent book is *House of Burnt Offerings* (Pleasure Boat Studio). Her work has appeared in *Cimarron Review, J Journal, Shenandoah, ZYZZYVA, Poetry, FIELD,* and elsewhere. Awards include an Eric Mathieu King Fund grant from the Academy of American Poets. <judithskillman.com>

Julene Tripp Weaver has a psychotherapy practice in Seattle, Washington. Her two poetry books are *No Father Can Save Her* and *Case Walking: An AIDS Case Manager Wails Her Blues,* containing writing from her work through the heart of the AIDS epidemic. She is widely published in journals and anthologies. <julenetrippweaver.com>

Julie Valin has been writing poetry since the first Loverboy album came out. She is an editor, book designer, and co-publisher of the celebrated after-hours poetry press, Six Ft. Swells. Her mission: to reach people who think poetry is for other people, and show them that it is for everyone. <TheWordBoutique.net>

Nine-time Pushcart-Prize nominee and National Park Artist-in-Residence, **Karla Linn Merrifield** has twelve books to her credit; the newest is *Bunchberries, More Poems of Canada*, a sequel to *Godwit: Poems of Canada*. She is assistant editor and poetry book reviewer for *The Centrifugal Eye*. <karlalinn.blogspot.com>.

Kate Wells is a high school English teacher at Charter University Prep in El Dorado County. She actually plays the violin. Not well, but there you go. She has been published in *Rattlesnake Review*, *Ash Canyon Review*, and *Albatross*.

After growing up in Logan, West Virginia, **Kathleen Corcoran** crossed the mountains to teach in Nigeria where she met her Irish husband-to-be. They settled in Maryland, both teaching at McDonogh School in Owings Mills. A Pushcart Prize nominee, her publications include *Naugatuck River Review*, *Baltimore Review*, and *Persimmon Tree*. <kcorcoran@mcdonogh.org>

Katy Brown, a retired Social Worker, poet, and photographer, whose work appears online and in numerous journals and anthologies has won a ton of impressive awards in various competitions; has twice been nominated for the Pushcart Prize. She grew up with hawks, rattlesnakes, and an older brother. <kbrown4081@aol.com>

Kenneth Salzmann's work has appeared in such anthologies as *Child of My Child: Poems and Stories for Grandparents*, *Beloved on the Earth: 150 Poems of Grief and Gratitude*, and *Riverine: An Anthology of Hudson Valley Writers*. He lives in Woodstock, NY, and Ajijic, Mexico, with his wife, editor Sandi Gelles-Cole. <kensalzmann@gmail.com>

Leah Mueller resides in Tacoma, Washington. Her work has appeared in *Blunderbuss*, *Origins Journal*, and *Sadie Girl Press*, as well as many anthologies. She is the author of a chapbook, *Queen of Dorksville* and two full-length books, *Allergic to Everything* and *The Underside of the Snake*. <wackypoetlady.blogspot.com>

Lennart Lundh is a poet, short-fictionist, historian, and photographer. His work has appeared internationally since 1965. Len started (and stopped) playing trumpet in 1959. <lenlundh@aol.com>

Linda Ferguson is an award-winning writer of poetry, fiction and essays. Her poetry chapbook, *Baila Conmigo*, was published by Dancing Girl Press. She also teaches creative writing for adults and children. She can't sing, but her son is teaching her how to play the piano. <bylindaferguson.blogspot.com>

Linda Goulden sings in a choir whose eclectic repertoire includes settings of some of her poems, others appearing on-line, in magazines (*Magma*), in anthologies (Emma Press) and in competitions (Poets and Players).

Lynn M. Knapp is a poet, memoirist, teacher, and musician. Her poetry has appeared in *The Burden of Light* (2014), *Poeming Pigeons* (2015), *The Lost River Review* (2015), and online at the Museum of Northwest Art in La Conner, Washington. She lives in the Pacific Northwest. <lknapp094@gmail.com>

Marilyn Johnston is an Oregon writer and filmmaker. *Red Dust Rising*, her collection of poems about a family's healing from war, was nominated for a Pushcart Prize. She is a writing instructor in the Artists in the Schools Program, primarily working with incarcerated youth.

Marj Hahne is a freelance editor and writing teacher, a 2015 MFA graduate from the Rainier Writing Workshop, and the founder-director of The Avocado Sisterhood, a membership organization for women writers. Her poems have appeared in literary journals, anthologies, art exhibits, and dance performances. <MarjHahne.com>

Mark Kerstetter steals time away from restoring an old house in Florida to write poems and make art out of wood salvaged from demolition sites. His poems have appeared in *Jerry Jazz Musician, Evergreen Review, Connotation Press* and other journals. Mark is the former poetry editor of *Escape Into Life*. <marktkerstetter.wordpress.com>

Michael T. Coolen is a pianist, composer, actor, performance artist, and writer. His works have been published widely, including the Oregon Poetry Association and *Clementine Poetry Journal*. He is also a published composer, with works performed around the world, including at Carnegie Hall, MoMA, and the Christie Gallery in New York.

Nancy Haskett is a retired educator who lives in Modesto, CA. She has been published in *Homestead Review, Miller's Pond, Iodine Press*, and many others. She loves to read, watch baseball (Go, Giants!), and spend time with her three grandchildren when she's not writing poetry!

A prize-winning children's author (*Thelonious Mouse*) and poet addicted to jazz and swimming, **Orel Protopopescu** won the Oberon poetry prize in 2010. *What Remains* (2011), a chapbook, followed. *A Word's a Bird* (top 10 SLJ, 2013), her animated, bilingual poetry ebook is now available as a free download. <orelprotopopescu.com>

Once a rootless wanderer, once a New Yorker, **Peter D. Goodwin** now resides in Maryland, close to the Chesapeake Bay, writes poetry while unwillingly providing succulent treats for deer, rodents, birds and insects.

Peter Larsen has written doggerel since he was nine. A retired wood sculptor, he now attempts to limn, manipulate, and bully words into structures of sound. Occasionally his fondness for Ogden Nash leaks through. <woodendane@juno.com>

Robert Coats has been writing poetry for 40 years. His work as an environmental scientist takes him outdoors and sometimes provides inspiration and material. His poems have appeared in *Orion*, *Freshwater* (Pudding House Publications) and a full-length book *The Harsh Green World* (Sugartown Publishing). <coats@hydroikos.com>

Rosemary Douglas Lombard, university music lit teacher, naturalist, prize-winning writer, and ethologist/"turtle tutor," explores the potential of turtle minds. *Turtles All the Way: Poems* (Finishing Line Press) is forthcoming; *Diode's Experiment: A Box Turtle Investigates the Human World* is in progress. Her poetry has appeared in *Verseweavers*, *Blue Print Review*, *Work*, and elsewhere. <rosemarydlombard@yahoo.com>

A California girl who upped stakes to travel the globe nearly a quarter century ago, **Sandra Hanks** now lives in the Indian Ocean island nation of Seychelles. Radio presenter, newspaper columnist, writer and poet, she follows world happenings from a western-facing veranda and partakes in magnificent sunsets. <sandrahanksbenoiton.com>

Sarah Key has written eight cookbooks, essays on the Huffington Post, and numerous poems in journals such as *Poet Lore*, *Minerva Rising*, and *Tuesday: An Art Project*. She teaches writing at a community college in the Bronx. <sarahkeynyc.com>

Scott Thomas Outlar's most recent chapbook *Songs of a Dissident* was released through Transcendent Zero Press and is available on Amazon. His poetry collections *Happy Hour Hallelujah* (CTU Publishing) and *Chaos Songs* (Weasel Press) are forthcoming. <17Numa.wordpress.com>

Shahé Mankerian's manuscript, *History of Forgetfulness*, has been a finalist at four prestigious competitions: the 2013 Crab Orchard Series in Poetry Open Competition, the Bibby First Book Competition, the Quercus Review Press (Fall Poetry Book Award), and the 2014 White Pine Press Poetry Prize. His poems have appeared in *Mizna*. <baronshahe@gmail.com>

Shawn Aveningo is a globally published poet whose work has appeared in over 100 literary journals and anthologies. She's a Pushcart nominee, co-founder of The Poetry Box® and journal designer for *VoiceCatcher*. Shawn is a proud mother of three and shares the creative life with her husband. <redshoepoet.com>

Susan P. Blevins was born in England, lived 26 years in Italy, and now enjoys living in Houston, Texas, where she reads, writes and gardens with a passion. She loves cats, stimulating conversation and a good laugh. <spgblevins@mac.com>

Susana H. Case's newest and fourth poetry book is *4 Rms w Vu* (Mayapple Press, 2014). She is also the author of 4 chapbooks, one of which, *The Scottish Cafe* (Slapering Hol Press), was re-released in a Polish-English version, *Kawiarnia Szkocka*, by Opole University Press in Poland. <iris.nyit.edu/~shcase>

Suzanne Bailie is a playwright and a poet. Her short plays and monologues are produced across the world. Suzanne's poetry is included in many anthologies and online magazines. A couple of her favorite activities is drinking strong coffee, creating sculptures with hot glue guns and colorful donkey art.

Suzanne DeWitt Hall is a HuffPost blogger, a writer for *Merrimack Valley Magazine*, and author of *Rumplepimple*. She is obsessed with vintage cookbooks, and the intersection of sexuality and theology. <sdewitthall.com>.

Tiffany M. Burba is a poet and photographer living in Vancouver Washington. Tiffany has been published in *Ghost Town Anthology* Volume 2 (Printed Matter Press 2014) in *The Poeming Pigeon: Doobie or Not Doobie* and just released her first book of Poetry entitled *Meet Me Where I Left You* (Printed Matter Press 2016).

Todd Cirillo is co-founder and publisher of Six Ft. Swells Press. His poems have appeared in numerous literary journals, magazines and cocktail napkins everywhere. Music is a must in his world—he always has something playing on the stereo, in his heart or the streets of his beloved New Orleans. <piratetrucker@yahoo.com>

Toni Partington is a poet, editor, visual artist, and life coach living in Vancouver, WA. She co-hosts the Ghost Town Poetry Open Mic, coordinates Poets in the Schools, and is the author of two books of poetry, *Jesus Is A Gas* and *Wind Wing*. <printedmattervancouver.com>

Tricia Knoll is an Oregon poet who has a voice disability — so she hums a lot and tweets haiku nearly everyday. She will sing to trees upon request. Her recent book is *Ocean's Laughter* about a small town on Oregon's north coast. <triciaknoll.com>

Music has always been a big part of **Wayne Lee**'s life. He performed at the Oregon Shakespeare Festival as a dancer/musician, played first violin in a string quartet in Seattle for 22 years, and worked as a music critic for the *Washington Times*, *Seattle Times*, *Jazziz* magazine and other publications. <wayneleepoet.com>

Index of Poets

The following authors whose poem(s) begin on the annotated page number(s) are indexed by last name:

Anglin, JoAnn: 21
Arcana, Judith: 34
Aveningo, Shawn: 79
Bailie, Suzanne: 50
Barkman, Donna: 111
Barrington, Judith: 41
Belmont, David: 103
Blevins, Susan P.: 26
Brand, Gabriella: 47
Brown, Katy: 60
Burba, Tiffany M.: 123
Case, Susana H.: 117
Catlin, Alan: 40
Cirillo, Todd: 75
Cloyd, Janel: 97
Coats, Robert: 38
Cole, Diana: 32
Coolen, Michael T.: 15
Corcoran, Kathleen: 124
Cushing, Bill: 91
Dahl, Carolyn A.: 25
Dees, Diane Elayne: 56
DeWitt Hall, Suzanne: 35
Fenn, Jennifer: 33
Ferguson, Linda: 52
Frayer, Bill: 119
Gaines, Josh: 105
Garber, Brad G.: 120
Goodwin, Peter: 108
Goulden, Linda: 104
Grunseth, Annette L.: 53
Haag, Jan: 61

Hahne, Marj: 107
Hambrick, Jennifer: 58
Hanks, Sandra: 67
Harding Woodworth, Anne: 43
Haskett, Nancy: 65
Hope, Akua Lezli: 94
Huffman, A.J.: 78
Jibson, David: 112
Johnston, Marilyn: 39
Jules, Jacqueline: 83
Kerner, Helen: 95
Kerstetter, Mark: 100
Key, Sarah: 80
Knapp, Lynn M.: 118
Knoll, Tricia: 57
Larsen, Peter: 82
Lee, Wayne: 36
Leotta, Joan: 51
Linville, Cynthia: 73
Lockie, Ellaraine: 121
Lombard, Rosemary Douglas: 22
Luna, Christopher: 84
Lundh, Lennart: 90
MacLachlan, Jeffrey H.: 113
Mankerian, Shahé: 114
Martin, Carolyn: 23, 116
Maze, Jack: 24
McGurn, Eileen: 68
Meltvedt, Deborah J.: 49
Merrifield, Karla Linn: 69
Miller, Amy: 31
Miller, Jane: 46
Mueller, Leah: 62
Outlar, Scott Thomas: 16
Partington, Toni: 71
Post, Connie: 44, 63
Protopopescu, Orel: 98

Quaempts, Judith Kelly: 81
Rammelkamp, Charles: 115
Raphael, Dan: 101
Salzmann, Kenneth: 125
Savage, Claudia F.: 28
Schneider, Ada Jill: 30
Scribner, Christopher: 85
Skillman, Judith: 20
Spangle, Douglas: 122
Tennant, Colette: 55
Valin, Julie: 74
Was, Carol Taylor: 70
Weaver, Julene Tripp: 87
Wells, Kate M.: 37
Whitehouse, Anne: 18
Yolen, Jane: 110

About The Poetry Box®

The Poetry Box® was founded in 2011 by Shawn Aveningo & Robert R. Sanders, who whole-heartedly believe that every day spent with the people you love, doing what you love, is a moment in life worth celebrating. It all started out as a way to help people memorialize the special milestones in their lives by melding custom poems with photographic artwork. Robert and Shawn expanded on their shared passion for creating poetry and art with the introduction of The Poetry Box® Book Publishing.

The book you now hold in your hands, *The Poeming Pigeon — A Literary Journal of Poetry,* evolved from the first issue (*Poeming Pigeons: Poems about Birds*) Each semi-annual issue will have a unique theme, with Homer, *The Poeming Pigeon* mascot, taking flight to deliver poems to poetry lovers across the globe. Details and submission guidelines can be found at www.ThePoemingPigeon.com.

As Robert and Shawn continue to celebrate the talents of their fellow artisans and writers, they now offer professional book design and publishing services to poets looking to publish their collections of poems.

Feel free to visit The Poetry Box® online bookstore, where you'll find more books including:

Keeping It Weird: Poems & Stories of Portland, Oregon

The Way a Woman Knows by Carolyn Martin

Of Course, I'm a Feminist! edited by Ellen Goldberg

Verse on the Vine: A Celebration of Community, Poetry, Art & Wine

Poeming Pigeons: Poems about Birds

The Poeming Pigeon: Poems about Food

The Poeming Pigeon: Doobie or Not Doobie?

and more …

Order Form

Need more copies for friends and family? No problem. We've got you covered with two convenient ways to order:

1. Go to our website at www.thePoetryBox.com and click on Bookstore.

or

2. Fill out the order form. Email it to Shawn@thePoetryBox.com

Name: _____

Shipping Address: _____
_____

Phone Number: (____) _____

Email Address: _____ @ _____

Payment Method: __Cash __Check __PayPal Invoice __Credit Card

Credit Card #: _____ CCV _____

Expiration Date: _____ Signature: _____

The *Poeming Pigeon — Poems about Music*

# of Copies: _____

x $15.00: _____

Plus Shipping & Handling: _____
($3 per book, or $7.95 for 3 or more books)

Order Total: _____

Thank You!

www.ingramcontent.com/pod-product-compliance
Lightning Source LLC
LaVergne TN
LVHW011838060526
838200LV00054B/4086